Backfire

*How the Ku Klux Klan Helped
the Civil Rights Movement*

David Chalmers

ROWMAN & LITTLEFIELD PUBLISHERS, INC.
Lanham · Boulder · New York · Oxford

ROWMAN & LITTLEFIELD PUBLISHERS, INC.

Published in the United States of America
by Rowman & Littlefield Publishers, Inc.
A Member of the Rowman & Littlefield Publishing Group
4501 Forbes Boulevard, Suite 200, Lanham, Maryland 20706
www.rowmanlittlefield.com

P.O. Box 317, Oxford OX2 9RU, United Kingdom

British Library Cataloguing in Publication Information Available

Library of Congress Cataloging-in-Publication Data
Chalmers, David Mark.
    Backfire : how the Ku Klux Klan helped the civil rights movement / David
Chalmers.
        p.   cm.
    Includes bibliographical references and index.
    ISBN 0-7425-2310-1 (acid-free)
    1. Ku Klux Klan (1915–   )   2. Civil rights movements—United States.
3. Racism—United States—History.   4. United States—Race relations.   I. Title:
How the Ku Klux Klan helped the civil rights movement.   II. Title.
HS2330. K63 C487   2003
323'.0973—dc21   2002014655

Printed in the United States of America

∞ ™ The paper used in this publication meets the minimum requirements of
American National Standard for Information Sciences—Permanence of Paper for
Printed Library Materials, ANSI/NISO Z39.48-1992.

Contents

Key Players

Sam Bowers   Imperial wizard of the White Knights of Mississippi

Richard Butler   Patriarch of Christian Identity's Aryan Nations, whose Idaho compound became the international meeting ground for white supremacists

Morris Dees   Cofounder and lead attorney for the Klan-fighting Southern Poverty Law Center

John Doar   Head of the Civil Rights Division and point man of the Justice Department in the South

David Duke   New-style Klan leader who combined National Socialism with elective politics

Henry Ford   Sponsor of *The International Jew* and Christian Identity's "Man of the Century"

J. Edgar Hoover   Legendary paranoid FBI director whom President Johnson pressed into a campaign against the Klan in the South

Lyndon B. Johnson   Pushed Public Accommodation, Voting Rights, and Civil Rights Acts through Congress

John Kennedy   Sought to get the civil rights demonstrators off the streets and out of the headlines and became converted to their cause

Robert Mathews   Terrorist founder of The Order who set out to begin the revolution

William Pierce   Head of the neo-Nazi National Alliance who laid down the terrorist plan in his books *The Turner Diaries* and *Hunter*

Robert Shelton   Longtime imperial wizard of the Alabama-based United Klans of America

Gerald L. K. Smith   America's leading anti-Semite who helped turn British Israelism into Christian Identity

George Wallace   Governor of Alabama

Michael Schwerner, James Chaney, Andrew Goodman, Vernon Dahmer, Michael Donald, Viola Liuzzo, Lemuel Penn, Cynthia Wesley, Denise McNair, Carol Robertson, and Addie Mae Collins   Died at the hands of the Klan

Anti-Defamation League (ADL), Center for Democratic Renewal (CDR), Center for New Community (CNC), and Southern Poverty Law Center (SPLC)   Leading anti-Klan organizers

· 1 ·

The Challenges of the 1960s

*A*mericans like to think of terrorism being connected with Europe, Latin America, or the Middle East, but one of the oldest living terrorist societies exists in the United States today. The Ku Klux Klan has been a loosely connected succession of racial terrorist societies in the United States from the post–Civil War Reconstruction era to the present. Almost one hundred years after the Klan was first brought to life, the Civil Rights movement of the 1960s confronted the Klan with the third major challenge of its history.

The first Klan came into being in the summer of 1866, organized as a social club by six ex-Confederate officers in Pulaski, Tennessee. From their college Greek, they took the word *kuklos* (meaning "circle" or "band"), added the word "klan" for its alliterative sound, and dressed in flowing robes and hoods for their mysterious nighttime initiations. The Klan's night riders quickly developed into a terrorist organization, spreading throughout the South. With ex-Confederate cavalryman General Nathan Bedford Forrest as its grand wizard, the Klan acted to overthrow the Reconstruction Republican state governments and enforce the subordination of the newly freed black people. Led by elites and drawing on a cross section of white male society, it did this through murders and assaults that totaled in the thousands. By the time that the national government intervened, the Klan had done its job. In white southern legend, the Klan is remembered as the savior of a downtrodden people from what they saw as the fearful disorder of black equality. The national government soon withdrew from a concern for black civil rights, and the "redeemed" South began a hundred years of racial segregation.

1

In the 1920s, the Klan reemerged, this time as the great fraternal lodge and would-be political engine of white native-born Protestant American nationalism. It was no longer narrowly southern,
and it enrolled literally millions of Klansmen and Klanswomen
across the nation. It helped elect governors, senators, and other
state and local officials literally from Maine to California. The Klan
came to town as social excitement and Protestant morality and reform. Prohibition was the great crusade, corrupt political machines
a useful issue, and Roman Catholicism the leading conspiratorial
threat to a Protestant, Anglo-Saxon America. The aura of violence
was an important part of the Klan appeal, although its actual practice was mainly in the South and Southwest. Scandal, corruption,
and struggles over money and power proved ruinous, the Roman
Catholic threat illusory. People came to believe that the Klan was a
civic disaster, and it rapidly declined. The Klan had no response to
the Great Depression but lingered on in the Southeast, principally
Georgia, Alabama, and Florida, as a violent enemy of blacks and
labor unions. World War II, gas rationing, and a large bill for back
taxes closed down the second Klan.

Brought back to life again in the Southeast after the war, the
Klan was strictly working class and antiblack, fragmented, but dangerous and not going anywhere. In 1954, the U.S. Supreme Court
decided that public school segregation was unconstitutional, and
the civil rights struggle moved out into the streets of the cities.
With Prohibition long since gone and anti-Catholicism, moral reform, and broader nativism almost all but forgotten, an anti-Negro
rage burned at the heart of the Klan's third great challenge.

The leadership potential in the South entered the battle for
segregation through more favored and somewhat subtle instruments such as the Citizens' Councils, state sovereignty commissions, federations for constitutional government, anti-Communist
crusades, and regular party politics. Economic and political pressure were espoused more readily than violence, but the Civil Rights
movement was in the streets, and more accustomed ways of control
and dominance were failing.

Would this be the Klan's moment? Could Klan violence blunt
and turn back an emerging black revolution? This was the chance
to gain the active role and the increasing membership that had so

long eluded it. Could the Klan recruit its legions by battling it out in the streets and build its own way to political power in the South? This was the Klan's opportunity and challenge, but it was fraught with peril. Not to fight would be to betray the history and meaning of the Klan, but to fight and lose would be to cast it into irrelevance. If the Klan eschewed violence, it was not the Klan, but when it acted like the Klan, what might be the costs that it would have to pay? The story of the 1960s was one of how Klan clubs, bombs, and bullets made a major unintended contribution to the civil rights revolution at an eventually increasingly costly price to Klans and individual Klansmen.

At the beginning of the 1960s, Klan violence had what amounted to a general immunity from arrest, prosecution, and conviction. Although most white southerners looked down on the Klan, it did have friends in power. When Klansmen met the "freedom riders" head-on in Anniston, Birmingham, and Montgomery, they might well have driven the Civil Rights movement out of the streets of the South. Instead, they called forth a new resolution of courage and activity among the young and prompted the reluctant involvement of the Kennedy administration and the national government.

Klan violence played an important role in the passage of the 1964 Public Accommodation Law and the 1965 Voting Rights Law. Klan violence in Mississippi forced the Johnson administration to turn a reluctant FBI into an effective Klan-fighting force, although prosecution sometimes had to wait until the death of J. Edgar Hoover or longer to release the crucial FBI files. Fear of Klan-produced anarchy and the possible employment of federal troops helped the Mississippi establishment minimally come to terms with the civil rights revolution. The failures of state courts led to a new role for the Justice Department and the federal courts, to landmark Supreme Court decisions expanding federal power, and to a new congressional civil rights law extending civil rights jurisdiction and protection.

By the 1990s, local immunity was gone. Old crimes (and new ones) were being settled in state as well as federal courts. More than thirty years later, state prosecutors and juries were sending the Klan killers of the 1960s off to die in jail and new murderers to the death chambers. In the first year of the new millennium, federal and state prosecutors combined to reopen the cases of the bombing of Birmingham's 16th Street Baptist Church and Klan killings in Mississippi. Still the Klan hung on, crowded to the side of a larger chaotic and violent upheaval of the end-of-the-century white supremacist world, which is set forth in the final chapter of this book.

Backfire tells four stories. The first, set against the rise and decline but not disappearance of the Klan, is how Klan violence forced the national and, belatedly, state governments into action. It tells the story of Birmingham, Montgomery, and St. Augustine, Florida, and of the murders of Mickey Schwerner, James Chaney, and Andrew Goodman in Philadelphia, Mississippi; Viola Liuzzo on the road to Selma, Alabama; Colonel Lemuel Penn on the highway outside Athens, Georgia; and Vernon Dahmer in Hattiesburg, Mississippi. It also tells the story of the Mississippi Klan, the campaign against the Jews of Jackson and Meredian, and the path through the courts of Alabama, Georgia, Mississippi, and the Supreme Court of the United States in Washington, D.C.

The second story is the four-decades struggle to punish the Klan murderers. The future Birmingham Church bombers, "Dynamite Bob" Chambliss and the Eastview Klavern 13 gang, are introduced in chapter 3. The conviction of the last of them in 2002 is told in chapter 17.

The third story is Imperial Wizard Robert Shelton's struggle to the top of the Klan world and his eventual downfall, related in chapter 16, at the hands of Morris Dees and the Southern Poverty Law Center.

In the fourth story, the final chapter takes American history on "the road to Armageddon's" violent racist emergence at the end of the twentieth century in which the Klan has lost its role as America's prime terrorist conspiracy.

· 2 ·

Laissez-Faire, Violence, & Confusion after the School Decision

*I*t was the Supreme Court decision against public school segregation on May 17, 1954, that gave the "Invisible Empire" a new impetus and environment for action. In a South marked by growing hysteria, the Klans burst into activity, and a resurgent proliferation of would-be leaders galloped about the landscape seeking support from old Klans and new Klansmen.

Shortly after the school decision, a red-haired, bespectacled paint sprayer at GM's Fisher body plant in Atlanta, named Eldon Edwards, revitalized the Klan in Georgia. Dr. Samuel Green, who had brought the Klan back to life after World War II, had died in the rose garden of his home in Atlanta, and his Invisible Empire fragmented into anarchy. Now, with old Doc Green's son Sam Junior acting as lawyer, Edwards got the state to charter his U.S. Klans, Knights of the Ku Klux Klan, which absorbed what was left of the old Association of Georgia Klans.

Compared to the others, the U.S. Klans did well, partially because Edwards talked tough and partially because he did not particularly practice it. Controlling a reasonably unfragmented kingdom in Georgia, he directed his primary efforts to expanding the frontiers of his domain. In competition with at least seven other would-be Klan organizations, Edwards's U.S. Klans reached a peak membership of perhaps between 12,000 and 15,000 followers early in 1958. No other leader could, at best, claim more than a few thousand.

Discipline and relative restraint, however, were not what many Klansmen wanted. Cross burnings, parades, motorcades, and

5

verbal violence were not quite enough. There were those who thirsted for a bit of the real thing, and there were others who took careful note of the money that the Klan brought in. Rivals reached out for Klan money and Klan power. Jesse B. Stoner was a slight, nervous man who had been orphaned in his teens and walked with a polio-induced limp. Thirty years old at the time of the Supreme Court decision, he had been an active Klansman for a dozen years. He had roamed through the world of Klandom, signing up recruits, running for Congress, or picketing the White House, one day opposing integration at Miami's Orchard Villa School and the next arranging to become head of a new Klan in Virginia. Wherever he was, Stoner filled the mails with pleas to do away with the Jews through joining whatever his present Klannish enterprise happened to be. Finally, by the 1960s, he had settled down in Atlanta, sharing an office with James Venable, the scion of a distinguished old Peach State Klan family and owner of the pastures at the foot of the Klan's sacred Stone Mountain. For probably as long as he has ever stayed in one place and tended to one task, Stoner handled the affairs of chiropractor Ed Fields's bitterly anti-Semitic National States Rights Party, which drew its inspiration from Adolf Hitler and his Nazi storm troopers.

Because of a World War I disability, Horace Miller necessarily lived a stationary life. He traveled instead on the wings of the Post Office, which carried his often-unintelligible newsletter and the application blanks of his mail-order Klan. When Klan material turned up in far portions of the globe among the neofascists in England or Austria, it usually began its journey from Venable's Stone Mountain or Miller's Waco, Texas.

The Bryant brothers, Arthur and Joseph, of Charlotte, North Carolina, were arrested in 1955 for sending their unsigned anti-Catholic and anti-Semitic literature through the mails. What the authorities found was not only a cache of dynamite and a rifle mounted over a truck windshield but also a pair of not unimpressive criminal records, extending from larceny and bad-check passing to juvenile rape and adult solicitation for prostitution.

When it came to talking tough, and maybe doing something about it, Alabama's Asa Carter ranked high on the list of Klan enterprisers in the mid-1950s. "Ace" was an Alabama farm boy who went off into the Navy and, unlike most Klansmen, got a touch of college, studying journalism at the University of Colorado. He worked as a radio announcer and eventually found his way back home again to make something of a reputation for himself around Birmingham as a critic of "rock 'n' roll" music. When he went into the Klan business, he took with him a "BE-BOP PROMOTES COMMUNISM" sign to put up on his office wall in the dingy ex–movie house out on Bessemer Road, where he made his headquarters. When he was fired for attacking the Jews on his broadcasts, he was ripe for new action. Sam Engelhardt, a big planter down in heavily Negro Macon County, was signing up businessmen, planters, bankers, and lawyers for the Alabama white Citizens' Councils. This left out the common man and Carter. To the ire of Engelhardt, who did not share his anti-Semitism, Carter began organizing the mechanics, farmers, and storekeepers into a Klan-like white Citizens' Council and then into a new Original Ku Klux Klan of the Confederacy.

Where the white Citizens' Councils elsewhere decried physical violence and Eldon Edwards generally tried to keep his Klansmen satisfied with strong talk and minimal night riding, Carter's followers eschewed moderation. One of his boys hit the headlines and the police blotters by leaping up on the stage of the Birmingham Municipal Auditorium to assault singer Nat "King" Cole. Four others got twenty years in jail for the turpentine-soaked castration of a black man, kidnapped for a Klan initiation ceremony. It was also some of Carter's boys who went up to Tuscaloosa to demonstrate against the admission of black coed Autherine Lucy at the University of Alabama. Early in 1957 at a meeting in his moviehouse auditorium, two of his Klansmen objected to Carter's one-man way of running things and asked for an accounting of the finances. Under such provocation, there was nothing that Ace could do but draw the revolver that he liked to wear strapped around his waist and "let 'em have it." Both wounded insurgents recovered, and the attempted murder charges against Carter were dismissed.

For a while, Carter hung about on the violent fringes of Klandom, and it seemed as though his dim star had just about flickered out, but Carter had a rare talent for reinventing himself. He had a way with words, and he would reappear in the 1960s as George

Wallace's speechwriter and author of Wallace's most memorable defense of segregation. A decade later, in a different place and with a different persona and a changed name, he was to write one of the most popular child's coming-of-age stories of his time, *The Education of Little Tree*.

Another brief stellar luminary in the world of Klandom during the late 1950s was Frederick John Kasper, who gave an Ivy League, intellectual note to Klan affairs. He was a slender, well-groomed young man from a middle-class family in New Jersey. After leaving Columbia University, he ran a small bookstore in Greenwich Village and idolized the aging literary hero and wartime propagandist for Mussolini's Italy, Ezra Pound. Kasper dated a black girl and had a good time in the free and mixed-race world of pseudobohemia, but this was not getting him anywhere. Pound told him that to become famous a man had to "do something," to take sides, no matter what the side was. Kasper picked white supremacy and stocked his new bookstore in Washington, D.C., with anti-Semitic literature and the writings of Pound.

Admiral John Crommelin was a masterful war hero who had been shot down when he bucked the Eisenhower administration brass over the decision not to build more aircraft carriers. When he launched a new civilian career by running for the U.S. Senate to save Alabama and America from the Jews, Kasper came down to help. There, Kasper met Carter, and the two informally teamed up to see what they could do to keep the schools of Charlottesville, Virginia, and Clinton, Tennessee, segregated. In a pamphlet titled "Virginians Awake," Kasper used his best Pound-like style to sum up the nature of the problem they faced and offered a few solutions:

> Jail the NAACP! Hang the Supreme Court Swine! Destroy the Reds! Save the White! Now damn all race-mixers . . . they stink: Roose, Harry & Ike. God bless Jeff/Jax & John Adams, also Abe. Loathe carpetbag, despise scalawag. Hate mongrel-izers (pink punks, hat-cheated high-brows, homos, perverts, freaks, golf-players, poodle dogs, hot-eyed Socialists, Fabians, scum, mould on top of the omelette). Myerization of News, liars for hire; the press-gang, degenerate liberals crying for petrefaction

of putrefaction, complainings-used to be blacker and richer, Social democrats, new dealers, Said Ben: Better keep 'em out or
yr/grand children will miss you. . . .

Death for Usurers, money monopolists, obstructors of Distribution (international finance, World Bank and Bunk, Unesco
currency, Federal Reserve racket, Barney Baruch's check book,
Schiff and Warburg finance Bolshevik refolooshun 1917, Leh-
man finances Newhouse $$ Birmingham News). (from "Virgin-
ians Awake" [Seaboard White Citizens' Council pamphlet],
quoted by James Rorty, "John Kasper's Moment of Glory,"
ADL Bulletin, December 1956)

Clinton was Kasper's great moment. As a result of a week of
door-to-door canvasing and haranguing, he turned the small com-
munity into a raging, seething mob town that only the Tennessee
National Guard could quiet. Clinton juries twice acquitted Kasper
of incitement to riot, but eventually a federal judge sentenced him
to a year in prison for contempt. Kasper never joined the Klan, but
the hooded knights initially took him to their hearts as one of their
own. While he appealed his several court sentences, he was a much-
sought-after attraction on the Klan circuit, particularly in central
Florida. However, when an investigating committee of the Florida
legislature offered testimony, including pictures, that Kasper had
consorted with black friends at mixed-race parties in New York
City, a reaction set in. Many of his former Klan friends disowned
him, although the newspapers in central Florida continued to re-
ceive occasional letters from parents who testified that that well-
dressed young fellow with such nice manners stood for what
America was really all about. When Kasper was released from jail, a
small group of friends, including Carter and Admiral Crommelin,
were there to welcome him, but his moment was past.

Of the Klan unsuccessfuls who splashed its name across the
headlines in the post–school decision 1950s, the most woebegone
was the Reverend James W. "Catfish" Cole of Marion, South Car-
olina. In 1956, Imperial Wizard Eldon Edwards had commissioned
him to organize North Carolina, but Cole soon came to feel that it
would be a shame to have to divide the spoils and power with any-
one else. Where the newly self-styled grand wizard made his fatal

error, however, was in his decision to carry Klandom into Robeson County, North Carolina. The Klan had operated there in the early 1950s until the county solicitor and the FBI caught some of them carrying victims over the state line for beatings. Solicitor Malcolm Seawell let the rest know that any more night riding meant first-degree burglary prosecution, which carried the death penalty.

Now, in 1958, Reverend Cole had a new wrinkle. The population of Robeson County was fairly evenly divided between three groups: whites, blacks, and the Lumbee Indians. In order to accommodate each of them, the county had a system of three-way segregation in schools, restrooms, and other places of public use. The Lumbees were a proud and prosperous people who had never lived a reservation life. It was widely believed that they were the descendants of the lost colonists of Roanoke. Some of them had blue eyes, and many of them carried old English family names, such as Drinkwater and Oxendine. For a number of years, they were known as "Croatans," after the single word found carved on a doorpost of the "lost colony."

Most of the Lumbees were farmers, but some had gone into business or served in city office. The town of Pembroke was largely Indian. While the Lumbees were unhappy over their own second-class status, there was one thing about which they felt most strongly, namely, the importance of setting themselves apart from black people. It was into this community that Catfish Cole's Klansmen brought their flaming crosses as a warning against Native Americans mingling with whites and in which they planned a big outdoor rally. On the appointed chilly January night, some fifty Klansmen found themselves gathered in the center of a field near Maxton while hundreds of armed Lumbees watched impassively from the road and the surrounding fields. Several of the Lumbees had streaked their faces with lipstick war paint, and one was wearing a souvenir warbonnet with "See Rock City" printed along its side.

At 8:30, when the meeting was supposed to begin, the Lumbees converged on the Klansmen, who were clustered fearfully beneath a single lightbulb suspended from a pole. As Klansmen desperately threw off their robes, an enormous Lumbee reached out and broke the bulb with the barrel of his rifle. The darkness was immediately lit by repeated bursts of light as Lumbees fired their guns in the air and news photographers flashed away. The Klansmen, trusting to wisdom rather than valor, fled.

There were a scattering of injuries and automobile tires riddled by shotgun pellets. A few bits of regalia, a Klan banner, and the public address system were left in the hands of the Lumbees. The state highway patrolmen moved in and arrested an armed and intoxicated Klansman whom they found lying in a ditch. Sheriff Malcolm McLeod warned the jubilant Lumbees to go home—that it was time to go home if they did not want to miss seeing *Gunsmoke* on television. Grand Wizard Cole was soon extradited to North Carolina and went to jail for incitement to riot. The press and magazines carried the story and pictures from coast to coast, and everyone laughed, except the Klan. The Kaspers, Coles, and Carters were doing it no good.

Thus, in the highly competitive world of free-enterprise Klandom, nearly a score of nonaligned Klans pranced across the landscape from Texas and Arkansas to the Carolinas. Despite the challenge of the Supreme Court school desegregation decision and the threat of integration, the Klans failed to grow and prosper. Part of this was the fault of the kind of leadership that the Klans drew. On the whole, it was appallingly bad. Most wizards and dragons, like Florida's Bill Hendrix, were concerned with the Klan as a money-making organization. Many, like the Bryan brothers in North Carolina, had considerable criminal records. Some, like Carter, were emotionally unstable and prone to sudden violence. Others, as shown most notably by the Reverend Alvin Horn of Alabama, were not inclined to practice the morality that they publicly preached. Most, like Reverend Cole, who took on the Lumbees, were prone to the unforgivable fault of bad judgment. Although they dreamed big, they thought small.

Across the South, it was much the same story. In Tennessee, Chattanooga had ignored the Klan during Reconstruction and cradled it in the 1920s. Although the size of the Dixie Klans was small, it was important in city politics. Chattanooga was a manufacturing and transportation hub. It combined a large industrial working class and an affluent upper class, but for a city of its size, the ordinary middle class was remarkably small. The Klan's following was to be found in the East Lake and Highland Park sections of the city, which stretched along the foot of Missionary Ridge from Rossville, Georgia, north to the Tennessee River. In 1962, the televised appeal from a reputed Klan spokesman helped elect a conservative Republican to Congress.

There were at least three competing Klans in Texas and Arkansas, claims of a revival in northern Louisiana, and only small crowds at rallies in Virginia, somewhat better ones in North Carolina, and even better ones in the western parts of South Carolina. In Florida, the major strength of the Klan had coalesced in the northeastern corner of the state. Socially conservative Jacksonville was torn between the polar roles of a modern expanding metropolis and the capital of crackerdom. With Mayor Hayden Burns preparing to bridge the two and cross over it into the governor's mansion, the citizens acquiesced at the polls to rural small-county control of state affairs and usually sent like-minded representatives to the legislature. While this did not augment the strength of the various Klans, it did create a world in which they could hold on to a marginal existence and occasionally score successes. One such success was the turnout for "Ax-Handle Saturday" in downtown Jacksonville in August 1960, when Klansmen assaulted blacks participating in a sit-in while the police watched.

The five would-be Klan empires that eked out a competitive existence in Jacksonville totaled less than 1,000 members. The most active was the Florida Klan, whose major Jacksonville unit, like so many Klans elsewhere, met under an assumed name. In this case, it was a fellowship club that convened in a rented hall on King Street, occasionally sponsoring meetings in the Duval County Auditorium or joining other Klans in rallies, institutes, and cross-burning recruitments. Although its numbers probably ran more than a hundred, only a dependable score or two were regulars. They gathered together on meeting nights, milling about informally while engaging in the usual Klan small talk of guns and killing. The hard-core membership included several retired ministers, a chiropractor, a plumber, car and jewelry salesmen, a high school student, and an occasional former politician.

It was in Georgia and Alabama, however, that the real fortunes of a Klan revival rested in the early 1960s. When Eldon Edwards was struck down by a heart attack, his successor was already waiting impatiently in the wings. Whereas Edwards had talked tough but sought to avoid going very far out on the limb with actual violence, Robert M. Shelton, a young rubber worker from Tuscaloosa, Alabama, appeared to be a man of action and seemed to be a real comer both within and outside the Klan ranks. He was a good organizer, he seemed to have friends in high places, and he was lucky. His luck came most primarily from the fact that his chief competition in Alabama Klan affairs, the Reverend Alvin Horn, had no luck at all.

In 1950, Reverend Horn and a group of Klansmen had gone after a Pell City storekeeper, Charlie Hurst, who was shot when he struggled to get away. Horn was eventually acquitted, but it was bad publicity. His wife, depressed over an operation, killed herself. As the father of six children, it was natural that Horn should seek a new helpmate, but when he finally found her, there was a terrible public to-do. The trouble was that Reverend Horn was forty-six, and his runaway bride was only fourteen. The police brought her back and lodged Horn in jail for contributing to the delinquency of a minor. Her parents planned to annul the marriage on the grounds of nonconsummation. When it became obvious that this was a losing argument, they let the marriage stand. All this did not appear to meet the moral standards that the Klan claimed it represented, and Shelton took over from Reverend Horn as grand dragon of Alabama.

The ambitious Shelton soon quarreled with Edwards, was expelled, and formed his own Alabama Klan. When Eldon Edwards died in August 1960, his boyish young protégé, Georgia Grand Dragon Robert Lee "Wild Bill" Davidson, succeeded him. Unfortunately, Davidson's nickname, which he earned with the attraction-getting buckskin jacket that he wore as an insurance salesman, was more indicative of appearances than performance. Wild Bill was too nervous and high strung for an organization such as the Klan. His inherited box-salvage plant in Macon, Georgia, was not doing well, and his rejection of both Shelton and the National States Rights Party as too fanatical indicated that his reign was going to be a pale copy of Edwards. The fact that he appointed Reverend Horn as his Alabama lieutenant was a commentary on

Imperial Wizard Robert Shelton

the quality of talent available to him. After an explosive meeting
early in 1961, his second in command, Calvin Craig, took the slim
Georgia legions over to Shelton. Since Mrs. Edwards was disin-
clined to relinquish her hold on the copyrights of the U.S. Klans,
Shelton continued to style his "only authentic" organization as the
United Klans of America. For the next thirty years, Imperial Wizard Robert Shelton was to sit atop Klandom's violent and slippery
pinnacle.

· 3 ·

Bombingham

The leadership potential in the South entered the battle for segregation through more favored and subtle instruments, such as the white Citizens' Councils, the Federation for Constitutional Government, anti-Communist crusades, and regular party politics. Economic and political pressure was espoused more readily than violence. The Klan leadership tended to come from people who might well be described as marginal fanatics and mercenary opportunists. Alas for the latter and for all sincere Klansmen, money was in short supply. It was obviously not going to come from the non-affluent membership of the Klan itself. Business communities did not support the Klan. A Klan sheriff usually meant the probability of a red-light district, gambling, drunkenness, absenteeism, and bad publicity. Businessmen in Clinton, Tennessee, and Little Rock, Arkansas, were frightened by the kind of men and passions attracted by racial violence.

Violence remained the way of the Klan. In 1959, the Friends' Service Committee, National Council of Churches of Christ, and the Southern Regional Council published a report on the first four years following the Supreme Court's school decision. It listed some 530 cases of overt "racial violence, reprisal and intimidation" and generally opined that law and order had been deteriorating in the South. The list of cases was a vastly mixed bag, and the various formations of the Ku Klux Klan were far from responsible for all of them, but there was case after case of the Klan's involvement in threats, cross burnings, floggings, and bombings.

An admittedly partial list of overt violence, much of it the work of the hooded knights, included the following:

15

6 black people killed;

29 individuals, 11 of them white, shot and wounded in racial incidents;

44 persons beaten;

5 stabbed;

30 homes bombed; in one instance (at Clinton, Tenn.) an additional 30 houses were damaged by a single blast; attempted blasting of 5 other homes;

8 homes burned;

15 homes struck by gunfire, and 7 homes stoned;

4 schools bombed, in Jacksonville, Nashville, and Chattanooga, and Clinton, Tenn.;

2 bombing attempts on schools, in Charlotte and Clinton;

7 churches bombed, one of them white, and an additional attempt on a black church;

1 church in Memphis burned; another church stoned;

4 Jewish temples or centers bombed, in Miami, Nashville, Jacksonville, and Atlanta;

3 bombing attempts on Jewish buildings, in Gastonia, N.C., Birmingham, and Charlotte;

1 YWCA building in Chattanooga and an auditorium in Knoxville dynamited;

2 schools burned;

In addition, 17 towns and cities were threatened by mob action. (*Intimidation, Reprisal and Violence in the South's Racial Crisis* [1959])

When the politicians pledged that the South would never integrate and officials and community leaders resisted openly and covertly by noncompliance and organized economic pressure, the example was already set. Society seemed ready to be saying "go ahead" at the same time it told the Klans that they had better behave. Communication within society is at best only partial, for the Klan's natural constituency did not listen to what community leadership had to say. The people who could send their children to private schools, who could move to a more expensive all-white neighborhood, who never ate at the lunch counters, and who were not likely to have to confront black people at their country clubs offered no competition for the Klan's cyclopes and dragons.

The person who was important, the sheriff, was popularly elected. Deputies, for whom any form of civil service was unknown, completely depended on him for their jobs. The sheriff and his deputies often came out of the same world that the Klans did. The sheriff was the power in his county. While no one could predict single episodes, violent Klan activity meant, at the least, that the sheriff was not concerned about preventing it.

While the southern attorneys general and governors condemned the Klan, which had not had a "look-in" in a southern statehouse since the grand dragon addressed Strom Thurmond's applauding South Carolina legislature in 1948, the Klan's sporadic cross burnings, beatings, and floggings continued. The new feature was the use of dynamite. Between January 1, 1956, and June 1, 1963, at least 138 bundles of dynamite sent clouds of smoke rising upward above the scarred racial frontiers between the black and white worlds. Black churches, newly purchased homes in a white neighborhood, the residences of white moderates or civil rights sympathizers, newly integrated schools, the YWCA in Chattanooga and the Knoxville auditorium in Tennessee, and synagogues in Miami and Jacksonville, Florida; Gadsden, Alabama; and Nashville, Tennessee, bared their wounds or collapsed into rubble.

Although the general response to the bombings was one of shock and condemnation, the dynamiter, Klansman or racial extremist, was outside the ordinary community and not affected by its feeling. A special police intelligence organization, the Southern Conference on Bombing, was set up in 1958 under the sponsorship of the staunchly segregationist Mayor Haydon Burns of Jacksonville to coordinate the efforts of southern law enforcement agents, but bombers were difficult to track down and even harder to convict. Would-be dynamiters were convicted in Charlotte, North Carolina, but despite a signed confession, others were acquitted in Montgomery, Alabama. In Atlanta, Klansman–Attorney James Venable successfully defended a group of National States Rights Party men against similar charges with the aid of character witnesses, including Klan Wizard Eldon Edwards, and an alibi provided during a period of "temporary lucidity" by an inmate of a state mental institution.

Although police efforts were not particularly successful,

explosives did leave fingerprints behind for the trained expert. Careful police work and a growing cooperation among the states and with the FBI, which had carefully infiltrated the most prominent fringe groups, promised some measure of control if only by promoting caution among the bombers. Only a portion of the dynamitings, though a large one, had been carried out by organized resistance groups such as the Klan.

In the free-enterprise world of dynamiting, two leading entrepreneurs emerged. They were the National States Rights Party's J. B. Stoner and the United Klan's Eastview Klavern 13. Stoner was a poor public speaker but a good hater. At a young age, he discovered the Klan and the "Jewish conspiracy," moved from Chattanooga to Atlanta, got a law degree from an unaccredited law school, and committed his life to forming anti-Jewish organizations and setting bombs. Willard Rose, who covered the South for the *Miami Herald,* told of a conversation in which Stoner was raging on about "the nigger this . . ." and "the nigger that . . ." "Why do you say things like that to me?" Rose asked him. "You know that I don't agree with you." "You're a white man ain't ya?" Stoner replied.

While Stoner was continually on the move about the South in the 1950s and 1960s, Eastview Klavern 13's home territory was Birmingham, Alabama. Bob Chambliss and Pops Blanton were Klan old-timers. In the 1920s, Chambliss belonged to Birmingham's then-mighty Robert E. Lee Klavern. He learned dynamiting as a quarryman and worked in the city garage, but he got into trouble for taking part in a Klan flogging, making threats, attacking a newsman, and rioting against Autherine Lucy at the University of Alabama. As black families began moving into white neighborhoods in College Hills and Fountain Heights, he helped College Hills become known as "Dynamite Hill" and Birmingham earn the nickname of "Bombingham." The police knew him as "Dynamite Bob."

Bobby Frank Cherry learned explosives in the Marines. Almost half a century later, on trial for the bombing of Birmingham's 16th Street Baptist Church, Cherry was identified from a photograph of men beating a black minister, Fred Shuttlesworth, who was trying to register his children at an all-white school. "Bopped ol'

Shuttlesworth in the head," Cherry boasted afterward, also commenting on a different assault that he had "split a nigger's head open." Cherry was part of Eastview Klavern 13's "action squad," along with Chambliss and Pops Blanton's son Tommy. As Robert Shelton was consolidating his hold on the Alabama Klandom, a beefy brawler named Gary Thomas Rowe Jr. joined Eastview Klavern 13 at the direction of his FBI handler and became part of the action squad.

Eastview Klavern 13 was giving Imperial Wizard Shelton problems. He did not like Chambliss and the Blantons hanging out so much with the National States Rights Party crowd. It was alright to hate the blacks and the Jews, but being friends with Nazis was downright un-American. Mainly, though, it was a matter of control. Shelton expelled the Blantons, and they gathered with Chambliss, Cherry, and a dozen or so others down by the Cahaba River, which they took as the name of their group.

Despite distractions, these were good days for Imperial Wizard Shelton. One splendid thing about being the Klan's top honcho was getting one's words (and face) in all the national magazines, particularly the sexy ones, such as *Playboy* and *Penthouse*. If what the American male wanted was sex and violence, Imperial Wizard Shelton could supply the violence. With a flow of words about "fluoridation," "kosher food," and the "United Nations" in his flat, toneless voice, he told *Cavalier* where he stood:

> The only thing for me is the Klan. The others may call a nigger a nigger all right, but do they call a Jew a Jew? The John Birchers may be all right for what they're trying to do, but do they talk about the Jewish conspiracy? Even the White Citizens' Council has plenty Jews in it. . . . Our aim is to educate the people to the conspiracy between Jews, niggers, and communists to take over the government. . . . We all know the nigger ain't smart enough to manipulate the moves he's makin'. It is the Jews who are back of this.

Despite similar concerns about Jewish conspiracy, Shelton had only contempt for George Lincoln Rockwell and his American Nazis. Rockwell had never amounted to much. "He don't believe in

Christ. I'm a Methodist," Shelton explained, "have a wife and three children; they're all Methodists" (quoted in Per Laursen, "The 101% American," August 1964).

The attention given to the Jews was particularly significant. One of the most pronounced aspects of the post–World War II Klan was its violent anti-Semitism. While this had long been a Klan theme, it had become increasingly strong. Without the resources to turn out their own propaganda, the Klans found a ready, inexpensive supply of literature available from professional anti-Semites, such as Conde McGinley and Gerald L. K. Smith. The tone was right, and the words soon became their words.

As the Klan turned more and more to anti-Semitic arguments and inspiration, the leadership of the two movements became more and more intertwined. Integration was denounced as a Communist–Jewish conspiracy plotting to overthrow white Christian mankind. Temple and synagogue bombings were described as attempts on the part of the Jews to gain sympathy; Eichmann did not really kill all those Jews, but "good for him" if he did. Hitler had the right idea. Arrested Klansmen were victims of Jewish persecution, and the "Jew-N" was to blame for the troubled state of the world. A Nazi salute was used in South Carolina rallies; Asa Carter's Klansmen dressed in storm-trooper outfits, and the Klan's friend, the violently anti-Semitic National States Rights Party, wore the Nazi "SS" insignia.

The success of anti-Semitism stemmed from the patness of the explanation it offered for the Klansman's anxieties: his fear of race mixing, his financial and social insecurity, and his xenophobia. He experienced some difficulty in picturing the hitherto docile black people, to whom he was accustomed, as being in intense revolt. The explanation of a Jewish conspiracy proved most illuminating. When southern governors denounced the black revolt as the product of Communism and troublemaking outsiders, Klansmen adopted similar theories of their own.

· 4 ·

Friends in High Places:
George Wallace

$\mathcal{A}$fter the Klan's fall from grace and power in the 1920s, only local scatterings remained from its once powerful network of political friends. Klansmen might be found on jury pools and among the ranks of city policemen and sheriffs' deputies in the South, but by midcentury only in Georgia and Alabama and in symbolic national politics did the Klan have a larger role to play. For politicians, cartoonists, editorial writers, and much of the general public, the Klan represented society's most violent racial extremism. To black Americans, even when it was not an immediate threat, the Ku Klux Klan represented all that was oppressive in their relationship with white America.

It is possible that Richard Nixon's first campaign to become president of the United States was a casualty of the symbolic power of the Klan image and of the intramural struggles among the Florida Klans. In September of the 1960 presidential election year, Bill Hendrix, the hardened veteran of many Klan wars, announced that he was for Arkansas Governor Orval Faubus, the unwilling nominee of the National States Rights Party. Since the bitterness between Hendrix and his fellow would-be Florida grand dragon, W. J. Griffin, was well known, the press went to see what Griffin thought about things. This put the Tampa private detective in an embarrassing position. Hendrix had endorsed Faubus first, and to tag along behind his rival was too bitter a pill for Griffin to take. He swallowed hard, cleared his throat, and proclaimed that he was for Nixon.

In October, in the third of the crucial Nixon–Kennedy

television debates, John Kennedy was questioned about the claims made by some of his prominent supporters that "all bigots will vote for Nixon." Kennedy replied, "Well, Mr. Griffin, I believe, who is the head of the Klan, who lives in Tampa, Florida, indicated in a statement, I think, two or three weeks ago that he was not going to vote for me, and that he was going to vote for Mr. Nixon." Having delivered his shaft, Kennedy went on to say that it was absurd to think that Nixon did anything but strongly disapprove of any such endorsement, a sentiment that Nixon was glad to echo. "I don't give a damn what Nixon said," Griffin retorted the next day, "I'm still voting for him." In an election in which Kennedy's narrow victory depended so heavily on the overwhelming margins piled up in Negro precincts in cities such as Chicago, perhaps Griffin's words helped make the difference.

The story was different in Alabama politics. Among the candidates for governor in 1958 were State Attorney General John Patterson and Circuit Judge George Corley Wallace. Patterson's chief political qualification was that his father had been murdered for attempting to clean up Phenix City, a red-light-district town across the river from Fort Benning and Columbus, Georgia. In the hysteria that was sweeping across the South in the wake of the Supreme Court school desegregation decision, the issue of race, always so close beneath the surface, became central. Patterson eagerly used it. His campaign manager was the banker Charles Meriwether, who had run Admiral John Crommelin's campaign, which first brought John Kasper and Asa Carter together. Although Patterson had earlier signed the southern attorneys general's resolution against the Klan, he now wrote to Imperial Wizard Bobby Shelton for support. The Klan endorsed Patterson and worked on his campaign. As he later told *New York Times* reporter Howell Raines, the Klan was "a factor to consider. . . . They can do you great harm; they can do you great good. . . . And of course, I wasn't about to run 'em off."

Judge Wallace, who had always treated black people with respect in his court, tried to turn the Klan issue against Patterson. Taking a bed along with him on the back of a pickup truck, Wallace would ask his audiences, "Where is John Patterson?" Then he would lift up the covers, peer inside, and call out "Who is down there between the sheets with you, John?" It was no use—Wallace was on the wrong side of the issue, and Patterson won, but Wallace had learned his lesson well. "I started off talking about schools and highways and prisons and taxes," he explained, "and I couldn't make them listen. Then I began talking about niggers—and they stomped the floor."

With Patterson victorious in 1958, Klansman Shelton's star was in the ascendancy. He was appointed Goodrich Tire Company's state sales agent and managed to land it a $1.6 million contract from the state. In time, relations cooled between Shelton, his friends, and his employer. Governor Patterson came out in early support of Kennedy's presidential hopes despite the fact that Kennedy was a Roman Catholic. Shelton told a Tuscaloosa courthouse convention of Alabama Klansmen that they "should stay away from Kennedy and keep an eye on John Patterson and Charles Meriwether," whom he claimed were tools of the Jews. While other Alabama politicians soon came to attack the Kennedy administration, Meriwether, from his new post on the Export-Import Bank, obviously was not too dissatisfied. Shelton, however, was soon separated from the Goodrich Tire Company in what they described as a reduction in force and he denounced as political persecution.

In 1962, George Wallace was elected to the first of his four terms as Alabama governor (five if you count the stand-in term of his wife, Lurleen). In the 1930s and 1940s, Alabama, one of the nation's poorest and neediest states, was the South's strongest New Dealer. As best they could, Governor Bibb Graves, Senators Lister Hill and John Sparkman, and a group of northern Alabama congressmen represented the interests of workers and small farmers and businessmen. Then came the Dixiecrat revolt in 1948, the 1954 school desegregation decision, and the civil rights revolution of the 1960s. Black demonstrators were out in the streets of the southern cities. As the leading Alabama historian Wayne Flynt wrote in *Alabama: The History of a Deep South State,* "When Northern liberals and Southern conservatives increasingly linked liberalism to race relations, the New Deal coalition began to unravel."

Elected governor in 1947 and 1954, Big Jim Folsom was running again in 1962. At six feet eight inches tall and 275 pounds, he was a maverick populist with a country manner and humor and a sympathy for the underdog, both black and white. He had been a formidable politician, but he had knotted himself up in corruption, sexual adventurism, and alcohol. And times had changed. George Wallace had been the southern Alabama manager of Folsom's successful 1954 campaign and a tax reform and education leader in the legislature. Now, having been beaten on the race issue by the conservative Patterson in the previous election, Wallace was again running for governor. He had learned his lesson well, and in 1963 he was sworn in as governor of Alabama.

Wallace told his speechwriter, Asa Carter, that he wanted an inaugural address that would make people take notice. Klansmen were accustomed to proclaim that as long as white men lived, "yesterday, today, forever," the Klan would continue to ride. Perhaps with this cadence in mind, Carter produced the words that drew local adulation and national attention to the Alabama governor. "Today I have stood where Jefferson Davis stood and taken an oath to my people," Wallace asserted. "I draw the line in the dust and toss the gauntlet before the feet of tyranny, and I say '*Segregation Now! Segregation Tomorrow! Segregation Forever!*'"

Wallace replaced State Safety Commissioner Floyd Mann, who had protected the lives of the "freedom riders." Mann's successor was Al Lingo, Wallace's violent racist crony, who had been his personal pilot during the campaign. Through Lingo, Wallace let the Klansmen know when their presence was wanted. Making trouble in the streets would give the governor an excuse to close schools, but Klansmen were to stay away from Tuscaloosa. There, at the University of Alabama, Wallace played out his nationally televised drama of refusal, with a chalk line drawn across the entranceway, before stepping aside to let the black students enter.

For Wallace's first presidential run in 1968, Carter joined with the leading anti-Semite propagandist, Willis Carto, to produce and distribute a campaign pamphlet, lauding him for standing up to the blacks and the liberal Communist conspiracy. In 1970, Wallace was running for governor again and would have another go at the presidency in two years. Having fallen out with Wallace, Carter also entered the list but finished badly with only 15,000 votes in the Democratic primary. No one had a majority, so there was a runoff. Wallace had come in second, and President Nixon and his advisers saw this as a great opportunity. If they could help defeat Wallace in Alabama, he would not be a threat when Nixon himself ran for reelection. With Nixon's operatives secretly giving $400,000 to finance his opponent's campaign, Wallace was in trouble. Carter rejoined Wallace and helped put together an underground campaign of false letters, anonymous phone calls and leaflets, and doctored photographs of interracial sex. Despite President Nixon's money, Wallace won again.

Almost a quarter of a century later, in a 1991 op-ed column in the *New York Times,* Dan Carter, the Wallace biographer and prize-winning Emory University history professor, continued the Asa Carter story under the headline "The Transformation of a Klansman." After a falling out with Wallace over the governor's "moderation," Asa Carter moved to Texas and reinvented his name, his livelihood, and his personal history. Borrowing from the name of the Confederate cavalry general and first grand wizard of the Klan, Nathan Bedford Forrest, for whom public schools are named across the South, Asa Carter became Forrest Carter and began writing western vigilante fiction. His first novel was made into his friend Clint Eastwood's movie *The Outlaw Josey Wales.* After Carter's death of a heart attack in 1979, his last fiction, a coming-of-age autobiography, became a prize-winning *New York Times* bestseller and a motion picture for children. True to the last to his prejudices, *The Education of Little Tree* is the story of a life that Carter never lived, growing up Cherokee in the eastern mountains of Tennessee and having escaped from a coercive "guv-mints" betrayal. When Carter died in a moment of alcoholic rage, he was unmourned by any member of his family.

With Lingo's state troopers to crack black heads in Birmingham and at Selma's Edmund Pettus Bridge, the Klan seemed hardly necessary, and George Wallace had a larger vision. He had understood the political possibilities of a white backlash. NBC newsman Douglas Kiker capsulized the perception: "Great God! That's it! They're all Southern! The whole United States is Southern!" In his *Politics of Rage: George Wallace, the Origins of the New Conservatism, and the Transformation of American Politics,* the historian Carter showed how Wallace shaped the race card into an attack on liberal government. "George Wallace had recognized the political capital to be made in a society shaken by social upheaval and economic uncertainty," Carter wrote. "The politics of rage that George Wallace made his own had moved from the fringes of our society to center stage." Whether Wallace really believed it did not matter. On the fringes of those fringes, there has remained room for the Ku Klux Klan.

· 5 ·

Freedom Riding

*T*he black lunch-counter sit-ins, "freedom rides," and massed demonstrations of the early 1960s offered a chance for the type of street-brawling violence in which the Klan excelled, and the enhanced specter of a black menace gave the Klan a degree of approval that it had lacked for many years. During the postwar 1940s and 1950s, the Klan had been mainly a status movement for its members. Only in its bombing along the racial housing frontiers in the southern cities did it act as a resistance movement. For the most part, merely by joining the Klan and participating in its verbal defiance, threats, and sporadic violence, the Klansman satisfied the urges that carried him toward membership.

The Klan revival in the early 1960s centered in Georgia and Alabama, the homeland of the twentieth-century Klan. In Alabama it became a Klan-style resistance movement that threatened to sweep the new Civil Rights movement off the streets of the South. Klansmen grabbed clubs and dashed off to the bus stations of Anniston, Birmingham, and Montgomery and to state university campuses at Athens, Georgia; Tuscaloosa, Alabama; and Oxford, Mississippi. Georgia Klansmen picketed the black sit-ins in Atlanta department stores and pushed state troopers aside to rally on Stone Mountain, but it was in Imperial Wizard Bobby Shelton's Alabama that the first crucial battles were fought.

For the most part, the Klan had not been active in the real black-belt counties of Alabama, where the black people made up most of the population but were seldom allowed to register and vote. It was in the center of the state that the Klans rode more freely than anywhere else in the South, except perhaps southwestern

Mississippi. If a rough four-sided figure were to be drawn to include Tuscaloosa, Birmingham, Anniston, and Montgomery, the major area of Klan activity would have been enclosed. Ringed in would be the major civil rights arena in Alabama. It contained the Klan's first line of defense against northern invasion in Anniston and Montgomery, where Martin Luther King Jr. and the bus boycott first made headlines. It contained the Birmingham battlegrounds of the freedom rides, the home of the Reverend Fred Shuttlesworth's Alabama Christian Movement for Human Rights, and the stronghold of Police Commissioner Eugene "Bull" Connor where King's marchers faced Connor's pressure hoses and dogs and where a campaign of racial bombing reached its crescendo at the 16th Street Baptist Church. It contained the Talladega residence of the Reverend Alvin Horn and the Tuscaloosa home of the University of Alabama and Robert Shelton's United Klans headquarters. Just to the south and west was Lowndes County, where Viola Liuzzo died on lonely U.S. Highway 80 on the way back to Selma after the Montgomery march.

From 1958 until his 1963 defeat at the polls and in the courts, Police Commissioner Connor came close to making his own law. In its simplest form, Connor's law read that blacks and whites were not equal in the eyes of either society or the police. By Connor's violent tactics and his tacit acceptance of those private operators who followed his example, encouragement was held out to Birmingham's Klansmen. Some 600,000 people lived in Birmingham's Jefferson County, one out of every five people in the state. Forty percent were black. In the bustling steel centers of Birmingham and nearby Bessemer, the black man was a possible economic competitor of the working-class white, and the Bessemer highway was as close as there was to a Klan highway in America. When it came down to harassment and beatings, Birmingham blacks claimed that it was sometimes difficult to distinguish between the Klansmen and the deputies. Also within the Klan's charmed geographic quadrilateral was the governor's mansion in Montgomery, where Alabama Governors John Patterson and George Wallace refrained from giving the impression that racial violence was completely distasteful.

In May 1961, CORE, the small, pacifist Congress of Racial

ATLANTA

GEORGIA

Decatur

Anniston

Birmingham

Tuscaloosa

Columbus
Phenix
City

Selma

MONTGOMERY

ALABAMA

Mobile

Equality, sent a group of thirteen whites and blacks on a bus ride through the Deep South to integrate interstate bus station waiting rooms. They notified the Department of Justice and the FBI of their schedule. This information was relayed to local Alabama police forces and through them to the Ku Klux Klan. When the first of the two buses arrived at the Greyhound station in Anniston, a mob pounded on the bus with clubs and pipes, smashed windows, slashed tires, and pursued it out of town. When the ruined tires brought the bus to a stop, the mob renewed the assault. A firebomb forced the passengers out into the mob. Fortunately for them, Alabama Public Safety Director Floyd Mann had placed a plainclothes state highway policeman on the bus. With gun in hand, the policeman held off the mob until other state troopers arrived to take the battered passengers back to Anniston. Treated in the reluctant local hospital, the passengers were besieged there until armed black rescuers arrived from Birmingham to bring them to safety.

There was no such escape for the second group of riders. Although some of them were beaten on the bus in Anniston, their

Burning "freedom riders" bus

Trailways driver managed to get back on the highway and drove on to Birmingham. There, another mob was waiting, with no police in sight. As FBI undercover informant Gary Thomas Rowe later testified, Public Safety Commissioner Connor had met with Imperial Wizard Robert Shelton and promised Klansmen fifteen minutes without interference. It had been Mothers Day, and all the policemen were visiting their families, Connor later explained. The Klansmen initially gathered at the wrong bus station, but a call from police headquarters sent them running to the nearby Trailways station. As the riders emerged from the bus, the Klansmen beat them bloody with fists, lead pipes, clubs, and kicks. The next day's newspapers around the world carried pictures of the beatings and the burning bus, and there was even a sympathetic front-page editorial in the segregationist *Birmingham News.*

In the attorney general's office in Washington, D.C., and at the White House, the Kennedys and their staffs debated what to do. Racial troubles would weaken the president in his upcoming meeting with the Soviets. The bus riders had to be protected, but using the Army or the National Guard would antagonize southern voters. A no-longer-friendly Governor Patterson was not going to commit political suicide by giving in to what he described as "the goddamned niggers," and the bus company refused to take the riders on to Montgomery. Eventually, despite bomb threats, the government got the battered "freedom riders" on an airplane and on their way to New Orleans.

But it was not yet over. A crucial decision had been made by the Nashville student nonviolent movement. In Birmingham, Reverend Shuttlesworth received a call from Diane Nash, who told him that Nashville was sending riders to take up the bus journey. Shuttlesworth asked her whether she knew that the freedom riders had been almost killed in Birmingham. "Yes," she replied, "That's exactly why the ride must not be stopped. If they stop us with violence, the movement is dead. We're coming. We just want to know if you can meet us."

"Tell them to call it off!" President Kennedy ordered, but no one could. Led by John Lewis, eight black and two white riders arrived in Birmingham. Connor put them in "protective custody" and after midnight dumped them back across the Tennessee line.

They contacted Nashville and returned. Robert Kennedy, the U.S. attorney general, persuaded Greyhound to provide a driver, and they were off to Montgomery. Alabama Public Safety Director Mann provided a convoy on the road. Police Commissioner L. B. Sullivan was to take over protection in Montgomery, but when the bus crossed the city line, there were no police anywhere. At the bus station, another mob was waiting. It beat them, men, women, and newsmen. President Kennedy's special representative from Washington, John Siegenthaler, lay on the pavement, bleeding and unconscious, while FBI men across the street took notes. Mann arrived on the scene. Firing shots in the air, he forced assailants back from one of the fallen students, and his highway patrolmen arrived in time to rescue the rest.

Through that night, the survivors, along with Martin Luther King Jr. and more than 1,000 mostly black people, were besieged in Reverend Ralph Abernathy's First Baptist Church by a violent white mob. Despite promises from Police Commissioner Sullivan, there were no police in sight. Federal marshals and prison guards, brought from the Maxwell Field Air Force Base, were beginning to lose their fight with the crowd when Governor Patterson finally declared martial law and sent in the Alabama National Guard.

With Klan leaders Robert Shelton and Alvin Horn and their lawyers, along with Montgomery Public Safety Commissioner Sullivan and the U.S. Justice Department representatives sitting before him, Federal Judge Frank Johnson Jr. issued an order against any more disorder. "If there are any other occurrences of this sort, I'm going to put some Klansmen, some city officials and some policemen, and some Negro preachers in the federal penitentiary in Atlanta," he said. Federal marshals, assigned to the judge's protection after the injunction, were to guard him for the next fourteen years.

Judge Johnson had been a law school classmate of George Wallace. Appointed to the bench by President Dwight Eisenhower, Johnson was a Republican from Winston County in the northern Alabama mountains. The people of Winston had remained loyal to the Union in the Civil War, and Johnson's great grandfather had been an anti-Klan sheriff during Reconstruction. Judge Johnson did not think much of discrimination, subterfuge, or demonstrations. The important civil rights decisions from the Montgomery bus boycott and Selma, through Morris Dees's Southern Poverty Law Center cases, emerged from his courtroom. Faced with a recalcitrant George Wallace and a segregationist state officialdom, at various times Judge Johnson took over supervision of Alabama's prisons, highway patrol, property tax assessment, mental health facilities, and public school systems.

Protected by the injunction and the U.S. attorney general's arrangements with the governors of Alabama and Mississippi, twelve freedom riders, accompanied by sixteen reporters, rode the bus from Montgomery to Jackson under the protection of the police, highway patrol cars, the FBI, helicopters, Border Patrol airplanes, and the Mississippi National Guard. President Kennedy's arrangements with the governor of Mississippi had not covered what was to happen after the arrival in Jackson. The freedom riders got off the bus in Jackson and walked into the "whites only" restrooms—and into a summer in jail and Parchman prison.

When more freedom riders kept coming, the president and the attorney general were frustrated and angry. The administration's purpose had not been racial justice but rather to get the demonstrators off the streets and out of the headlines. The Klan's furious assaults on the freedom riders had forced the national government to act. Diane Nash and the Nashville group had understood how important it was that the rides go on after Birmingham and the Klan not be left triumphant to claim control of the streets and able to say, "See, this is the way to do it." In the acrimonious negotiations behind the scenes with the Alabama governor, the national government had been forced to take a first major step toward becoming involved in the civil rights struggle. An angry Attorney General Kennedy received reports on the Klan–police role in Anniston, Birmingham, and Montgomery and the names of the Klansmen who had battered his representative, Siegenthaler, but the administration took no action.

As the next year's struggle over James Meredith's entrance into the University of Mississippi would show, the national government had no plan for dealing with violence. The bloodshed and the courage shown by the riders in Anniston, Birmingham, and Montgomery had drawn the attention of television, the press, and the nation. The Klan attack on the newsmen and photographers was an implicit recognition of how important that was.

The Kennedy administration pushed the Interstate Commerce Commission into ordering the desegregation of bus station facilities but offered no help for the imprisoned riders in Mississippi, who grew to some 300 over the summer. It did, however, quietly organize the privately funded Voter Education Project, under the direction of the Southern Regional Council, which it hoped would take the movement out of the streets and would be less confrontational. As the Student Nonviolent Coordinating Committee (SNCC) was to learn in the following years, the White Knights of the Ku Klux Klan in Mississippi did not recognize a difference. From the confrontation with the Klan mobs in Alabama and the experience of Mississippi's dread Parchman prison came the maturing of the SNCC as a committed civil rights assault weapon across the black-belt South.

As the freedom riders disappeared into the Mississippi jails, national attention turned to Martin Luther King Jr. and the Southern Christian Leadership Conference (SCLC). In 1963, the SCLC picked Bull Connor's Birmingham—the most unyieldingly big city in the South, with a reputation for racial bombing and police brutality—as their integration target. Connor's career as public safety commissioner had rested on support from lower-middle-class white voters and the "Big Mules," the industrial and commercial leaders of Birmingham. The freedom rider violence helped convince a more moderate sector of the business and legal community that Connor was bad business. The moderates were still segregationists, and Connor still held the police power long enough to make one last, unwitting major contribution to the civil rights drama.

Historians disagree over whether the SCLC strategy was based on provoking Connor. The campaign began badly with a hesitant black community. Only in the Montgomery bus boycott seven years before did King have the black churches united behind him. Not until the young people joined the marches and the sit-ins did the support rally. The arrests soared into the thousands as Connor's use of police dogs and fire hoses against the marchers made Birmingham the number one television news story.

In 1963, the network evening news was extended to a thirty-minute period, and the role of "anchorman" was created. For the first time, the news showed live action pictures, captured by newly developed lightweight cameras, that followed the demonstrators into the streets of the South and American soldiers onto the battlefields of Vietnam. Aided and pressured behind the scenes by President Kennedy, the business community moderates and the SCLC negotiated an agreement for the desegregation of downtown stores and the hiring of black salespeople.

Influential leaders, including the Big Mule iron and steel executives, and the Klan denounced the settlement. "A sellout by the Jew-dominated Chamber of Commerce," the Klan labeled it. Before a crowd of several thousand, Imperial Wizard Robert Shelton promised reprisals. Later that night, in an apparent attempt to catch King, dynamite bombs wrecked the home of King's brother, the Reverend A. D. King, and SCLC headquarters at the Gaston Motel, for which Connor had refused guard. The result was a night of indiscriminate black rioting and burning and indiscriminate beatings by Connor's police and the state troopers under the command of Al Lingo, whom the new governor, George Wallace, had appointed to replace the capable Floyd Mann.

With the news of the bombing and rioting, President Kennedy sent major Army units into Alabama on standby and was prepared to federalize the Alabama National Guard, which he later did in preparation for the admission of black students to the University of Alabama at Tuscaloosa. He continued to play an active behind-the-scenes role in attempting to persuade the economic leadership to support the Birmingham agreement, but he had come to believe that more was necessary. Up until now, the government had reluctantly responded to crises created by others. What was needed was a comprehensive approach to dealing with the whole problem.

In a process of involvement that had begun, against his desires, with the mob attacks on the freedom riders two years before, the president had come to commitment. On June 11, 1963, after Governor Wallace had announced his resistance and then stepped back, two black students entered the University of Alabama. That evening, in what is often considered his most eloquent television address, President Kennedy endorsed the Civil Rights movement and announced that he would propose meaningful legislation to Congress. Much more had gone in to this than actions of the Klan, but it had been an important part of an unpredictable unfolding.

Several hours later that night, Medgar Evers, Mississippi state leader of the National Association for the Advancement of Colored People (NAACP), was shot in the back from ambush and died in the driveway of his home in Jackson. In the black-belt city of Selma, Alabama, SNCC organizer Bernard Lafayette was also brutally ambushed, only to be saved from death by a shotgun-carrying black neighbor. Lafayette had been part of the first freedom ride into Montgomery. Now, he believed, the Klan had almost gotten him on its second try. Justice Department and FBI people, he related later, told him that he, Evers, and a CORE activist in Louisiana, who was opportunely out of town, had been targeted for a triple Klan murder: leaders of three different civil rights organizations—NAACP, SNCC, and CORE—in three different states—Mississippi, Alabama, and Louisiana. Contrary to Lafayette's belief, Evers was the victim of a solitary assassin, Byron De La Beckwith, who only later joined the Klan. There has been no evidence of a conspiratorial aspect to the murder.

A week after his televised speech and the murder of Evers, President Kennedy sent his proposed civil rights law to Congress. It had been almost a hundred years since the Reconstruction-era Congresses had enacted the first civil rights law. It had been passed over President Andrew Johnson's veto in 1868, but the Supreme Court had soon after declared it unconstitutional. Now, for the first time, a president of the United States had taken an active civil rights role.

The proposed law had many parts. The one that caught public attention was the prohibition of discrimination in public accommodation, "including all places of lodging, eating, and amusement and other retail or service establishments." There was no certainty—and much doubt—that Congress would pass it in any meaningful form. As SNCC leader John Lewis noted, it would not do much about voting rights and did not say anything about protection against violence.

The summer of 1963 seethed with extremist anger, particularly among the Klansmen and their political friends. The Birmingham

City Council repealed its segregation ordinance despite Klan pickets outside. Connor was now out of office, but he and other rejectionists and opportunists were busy. It took a joint injunction from all of Alabama's federal district judges and the president's federalization of the Alabama National Guard to override Governor Wallace's efforts to prevent token integration of the public schools. "Reporters for both state and national papers warned," the historian Wayne Flynt has written, "that Wallace's speeches tended to reinforce the violence-prone lunatic fringe of racists who had long sought to protest Birmingham's social order with bombs and guns." Such warnings, Flynt continued, "fell on deaf ears."

Early in the morning of Sunday, September 15, a fifty-nine-year-old city auto mechanic named Robert Chambliss, known to the police as "Dynamite Bob," and three fellow Klansmen from Birmingham's Eastview Klavern 13 placed a large dynamite bomb against the basement wall of Birmingham's black 16th Street Baptist Church. The firing mechanism was attached to a fishing float in a slowly leaking bucket. When the water drained out, the float settled, and the circuit was connected. The dynamite exploded at 10:22 that morning and killed four young girls—Addie Mae Collins, Cynthia Wesley, and Carole Robinson, all fourteen years old, and Denise McNair, eleven—who were getting ready to be ushers at the morning service. The fishing float was found a block away by the FBI.

·6·

The Long Hot Summer

*I*n the fall of 1963, with characteristic irony, President John Kennedy cautioned his staff not to be too critical of Alabama Governor George Wallace. "After all," the president commented, "he has done a lot for civil rights this year." Although it was painful to all involved, the same could be said of the Ku Klux Klan.

Kennedy had become president without a plan or a major concern for civil rights. It was not on his agenda. He believed that discrimination was wrong and that it would change over time, as it had for the Irish. He saw civil rights as a matter of politics, not morality, and the politics of the situation was that he did not wish to lose the support of the southern senators, congressmen, and white voters. The way that his Justice Department and the new head of its Civil Rights Division, Burke Marshall, read the Constitution was that race relations was a matter of state jurisdiction. The national government had no power to police the South and, short of a situation that needed the U.S. Army, had no forces adequate to undertake it. Attorney General Robert Kennedy was moved by a rising moral passion, but he saw the situation the same way. The administration's policy was to do what it could by influence, negotiation, and the filing of law suits. J. Edgar Hoover's FBI worked closely with southern police departments and shared their attitudes. While it had investigated the recent spate of southern bombings, the FBI did not hire black agents, did not intervene in racial conflict, and considered the Civil Rights movement and Martin Luther King Jr. to be dangerously subversive.

The pressure of the Civil Rights movement in the streets of the southern cities and the violence of the Klan and others forced the

Kennedy administration to become involved. Often not knowing whether it was more angry at the civil rights leaders than at the southern governors, sheriffs, police chiefs, and the Klan, the administration had been forced to seek federal court injunctions and to use federal marshals, federalized state national guards, and the U.S. Army to protect bus riders, enroll college students at the Universities of Mississippi and Alabama, and maintain order in the streets. The national commitment grew. The Birmingham campaign produced the first meaningful civil rights law since Reconstruction, and President Lyndon Johnson pushed it through Congress in the name of the fallen president. The violent activities of the Klan played an important role in producing this changing national commitment.

The major problem that continued to face and baffle the hooded knights was what to do about the civil rights revolution that was taking place all around them. The Klansman was sworn to resist it. He had pledged himself, in mystic oneness with his fellow Klansmen and in the mirror of his own self-respect, to succeed by whatever means. The Klansman's traditional and cultural way was violence—"to get a little bit of action," as Klansmen liked to describe it. When he did, he was particularly vulnerable. Whether his violence was spontaneous or carefully planned, the police and the FBI, if they wished to do so, knew where to look. There was too much talk, too many Klansmen were in on a secret, and, as has been the way since the days of Klan trials in Reconstruction South Carolina, Klansmen under pressure told on each other.

The Klans, therefore, successfully turned to more than sporadic violence only where popular and police sentiment granted them a high degree of local immunity, where lawmen did not interfere and often joined, and where judges and juries did not indict, convict, or hand down serious sentences. During the long hot summer of 1964, Klansmen found such places in Bogalusa, Louisiana; southwestern Mississippi; northern Georgia; and St. Augustine, Florida. These efforts had their price for the Klan, as did road adventures in Madison County, Georgia, and the next year in Alabama's Lowndes County. In the changing world of the 1960s, doing what Klansmen liked to do best helped bring about federal intervention, new national civil rights laws, trials in less sympathetic federal courts, and, eventually, guilty verdicts from local juries.

At a Klan rally in the fall of 1963 just outside St. Augustine, the Klan's string-tie, traveling evangelical friend, Connie Lynch, had successfully heated up his audience with cries for blood. "I'll tell you something else," he had said. "You've got a nigger in St. Augustine ought not to live . . . that burr-headed bastard of a dentist. He's got no right to live at all, let alone walk up and down your streets and breathe the white man's free air. He ought to wake up tomorrow morning with a bullet between his eyes. If you were half the men you claim to be," he harangued his listeners, "you'd kill him before sunup."

After his oratory had moved everyone more than an hour closer to sunup but without producing any blood, Lynch turned the platform over to his Jacksonville Klan host, and the crowd started to drift away. Suddenly, there were cries from the woods of "Niggers! Niggers!" and four black men, including the dentist Robert Hayling, who had been trying to spy on the meeting, were dragged forward at gunpoint. As the Klansmen began to beat them and cry for their mutilation and death, a spectator in the crowd slipped away and called the sheriff, who arrived in time to rescue the captives and arrest four Klansmen. Local juries found the Klansmen innocent of assault and battery but convicted the victims of attacking the Klansmen. In a right-thinking community like this, a useful organization such as the Klan might have a real future.

There was, however, a serious problem. Since the 1920s, one of the patriotic duties of the Klan had been to protect America from Roman Catholic subversion, and rural Klan fundamentalists still occasionally preached the anti-Catholic evangels from Klan platforms. The old Spanish town of St. Augustine was primarily Catholic, which on the surface would have made it an unlikely field for the sowing of the Klan seed. However, St. Augustine faced a greater peril in the upward black push for equality. This in itself was distasteful, and the citizens of St. Augustine had learned from years of education by the John Birch Society, the Dan Smoot Report, the Florida Coalition of Patriotic Societies, and a succession of patriotic speakers that Communism lay behind the Civil Rights movement. It was not without justification that the mayor could boast that there was "more awareness of Communism" in his community than in the rest of Florida.

In the face of this more serious menace, Jacksonville Klansmen closed ranks with young Catholics from St. Augustine's Minorcan community. The local activists, belonging to what an observant newspaperman called "the shirt-tail and mud-flap school of social expression," were led by Holsted "Hoss" Manucy, whose curly sideburns, black cowboy hat, and impressive brawny girth were to become as famous symbols of resistance as Connie Lynch's jutting jaw and string tie and Birmingham Police Commissioner Eugene "Bull" Connor's dogs.

The city of St. Augustine, on the eve of its quadricentennial celebration, drew its life from the tourists who came to view the preserved and re-created buildings and monuments of its Spanish origins. In many ways, St. Augustine observed a greater degree of racial politeness than hundreds of other southern towns. Having gone this far, however, the white community was determined that it would go no further. The black community, led by Dr. Hayling, was resolved that there was further to go. The white community leaders refused to meet with black leaders and talk things over. The mayor declined to appoint a biracial commission on the grounds that St. Augustine had no racial problems. The Florida Advisory Committee of the U.S. Civil Rights Commission reported that with the breakdown in communication between the communities, conditions were "considerably worse than in most, if not all, other cities in the state."

Black organization and demands brought threats of violence, economic pressure, beatings, and cries of police brutality. Shots were fired into Dr. Hayling's home, and a young member of Manucy's Ancient City Hunting Club was shot and killed as he rode with friends, shotguns in hand, through the black district. St. Augustine was beginning to make the newspapers. Sheriff L. O. Davis announced that he was not in the market for any black votes. "I used the word 'nigger' so they would know I meant it," he explained.

Black leaders turned from the National Association for the Advancement of Colored People to the Southern Christian Leadership Conference (SCLC) and asked Martin Luther King Jr. to come and take charge of their campaign. A civil rights bill was being debated in Congress, and St. Augustine offered the opportunity to create public pressure. When Mrs. Malcolm Peabody, the wife of a retired Episcopal bishop and mother of the governor of Massachusetts, was arrested as part of a mixed group seeking service in the downtown Monson Motor Lodge restaurant on Bay Street, it was national news.

By the latter part of May, there were nightly speeches and prayers in the black churches, after which columns of singing demonstrators formed to march on the Plaza de la Constitution in the center of town. Sit-ins began at the Monson Motor Lodge. Klansmen from Jacksonville's tough militant knights turned up for active duty. So, too, did longtime Klansman–lawyer J. B. Stoner, whose skills with dynamite and in defending dynamiters gave him particular prestige in Klan circles. Stoner was not much of an orator, but the Reverend Connie Lynch was among the best. Ever on the move from coast to coast and organization to organization, with an uncanny sense of where his services might be needed, he arrived in his pink Cadillac to help prepare the defenses against "Martin Lucifer Coon" and the "Jew conspiracy" of race mixing. Demonstrators who violated undesirable guest and trespass laws in local restaurants and churches were carted off to jail, penned out in the broiling June sun during the day, and often locked in a sweatbox cell at night while SCLC officials scoured the ranks of its members and friends to send new waves to fill the jails.

Marchers exhorted themselves and each other to refrain from striking back and formed ranks to face barrages of bricks, clubs, and blows from Klansmen, and Manucy's "raiders" gathered in the plaza. Receiving no orders to the contrary from St. Augustine's business leaders, Sheriff Davis's officers refrained as long as possible from interfering. Angry segregationists turned their particular attention to white marchers and news photographers, and Manucy picked up a little change on the side by selling protection to UPI and ABC reporters.

Town officials, police, integration lawyers, and state officials wrangled before Federal District Judge Bryan Simpson as to whether nighttime processions should be banned or permitted. Judge Simpson pressed the sheriff to maintain order and prevent violence. Inspecting a list of the sheriff's new deputies, the judge exploded when he came to the name of Holsted R. Manucy, whose civil rights were forfeited when Judge Simpson had previously sentenced him for bootlegging.

King and the SCLC appealed for supporters to come to St. Augustine. Individuals and groups, rabbis and ministers, white students and college professors, and black teenagers went to jail. Ex-Deputy Manucy's raiders tailed out-of-state cars and exchanged reports through citizens-band radios. Sentinels stationed at St. Augustine Beach called in carloads of reinforcements who came roaring across the sand with Confederate flags flapping, and club-wielding whites plunged into the surf after the racial interlopers. When Klansmen and segregationists paraded through their district, black people lined the sidewalks singing, "I love everybody." Curious spectators turned out nightly to watch Klan and black meetings, but the tourists, on whom St. Augustine depended for its economic life, had practically disappeared. Despite the newspapermen and state police officials who piled into the motels, business was suffering badly.

The scene of the daily conflicts shifted from the old shedlike slave market in the plaza to the Monson Motor Lodge to the surf of St. Augustine Beach and then back again. The governor's police maintained order for a few days until the Klansmen and raiders discovered that Sheriff Davis seldom booked them and that bonds for the attackers were rarely set above $25. Bail for those participating in sit-ins ran into the thousands of dollars, and Stoner and his Klansmen lounged about on the front steps of the jail. As the assaults on marchers and wade-ins reached their peak, Klansmen and raiders broke through police lines. Beatings and injuries became more severe.

King was arrested at the Monson Motor Lodge and then removed to a safer jail in nearby Jacksonville. He was bailed out in order to receive an honorary degree at Yale and then returned to St. Augustine again. When five black and two white integrationists jumped into the Monson Motor Lodge swimming pool, the manager James Brock could take it no longer. "I can't stand it, I can't stand it," he wept. Brock and many of the other small businessmen were trapped in the middle. Although a convinced segregationist,

Brock was willing to open up his establishment if required by law or requested by business leaders. He dared not be first. As he later explained it, "If I integrated, there wouldn't be more than one Negro a month registered at the motel, but the first night I integrated, all my windows would be busted in."

Community leaders who had been willing to countenance violence against black people and integrationists found that they were now unable to control it or turn it off, and state officials publicly agreed that St. Augustine businessmen must share the blame for it all. Appearing on national television with Lynch and Stoner, a prideful Manucy was asked whether he thought the trouble would continue in St. Augustine. In a booming voice that must have sent shivers down the spines of local businessmen, he happily replied, "Oh yes, there is going to be trouble for a *long* time!"

After a painfully bloody and highly publicized month, Governor Farris Bryant announced that he had appointed a secret biracial commission (which he had not), and the passage of the Public Accommodation Law managed to bring an uneasy peace. Pressure from the Klan and John Birch remained strong. Although local hotels and restaurants had agreed to comply, they held back. After a firebomb was thrown through the window of the Monson Motor Lodge's restaurant, they resegregated, and it took the stern hand and careful guidance of Judge Simpson to prevent more than sporadic violence. Klansmen Stoner and Lynch were arrested for illegal cross burning, and the court ordered Stoner to withdraw his National States Rights Party pickets from in front of integrated establishments. Manucy managed to stay in the news by mistakenly turning in a Klan bomber in the belief that he was going to get a reward for helping capture the union dynamiter of the strike-bound Florida East Coast Railroad. Himself facing the courts yet again in the fall, Manucy changed his mind after an hour's meditation in jail and supplied a list of the members of his Ancient City Hunting Club.

On July 11, 1964, a little more than a week after things began to settle down in St. Augustine, they flared up in Mississippi and Georgia. Just as FBI Director J. Edgar Hoover had arrived in Jackson, Mississippi, Lieutenant Colonel Lemuel Penn and several fellow officers were returning home from summer army reserve training at Fort Benning, Georgia. Penn, who was director of adult and vocational education for the District of Columbia, had come safely through World War II in the Pacific, but he was a black, and conditions were unsettled on the roads passing through Clarke County, home of the University of Georgia and of the violent Athens Klavern 244 of the United Klans of America. The Athens Klansmen had been beating local blacks and harassing and shooting up motorists without interference from the police. Colonel Penn and his friends had loaded up with food and soft drinks and planned to drive through Georgia as quickly as possible. The three Klansmen on road patrol noted the District of Columbia license plates and decided that this was part of a rumored civil rights invasion. The Klansmen pulled alongside and emptied their shotguns. Colonel Lemuel Penn's luck had run out.

For a while it looked as though that of the Klansmen would follow suit. FBI men moved in and offered rewards. Klansmen talked, and the driver of the car confessed. Conviction turned out to be more difficult. Since murder was not a federal crime, it was up to Georgia to prosecute. The state did its best, but it was perhaps asking too much for a jury from a rural Georgia county to decree the execution of their neighbors for the killing of a black man. The defense attorney made the most of this, telling the jury that the president had sent hordes of federal men swarming into Georgia ordered to bring back "white meat." "Never let it be said," he continued, "that a Madison County jury converted an electric chair into a sacrificial chair on which the pure flesh of a member of the human race was sacrificed to the savage revengeful appetite of a raging mob." The jury found the Klansmen innocent, and the sheriff stepped up to offer his congratulations. The best that the government could do was to hope that a charge of a lesser violation of civil rights might stick in the federal court.

· 7 ·

Mississippi

$\mathcal{A}$lthough the summer was hot in Florida and Georgia, it was even hotter and longer in Mississippi. Some of the "freedom riders" had stayed on after Parchman prison in 1961. They worked with leaders of the National Association for the Advancement of Colored People (NAACP), including Medgar Evers, Aaron Henry, E. W. Steptoe, and Vernon Dahmer, to register black voters, attracting young students and teenagers and determined women. As bad as Alabama was, Mississippi was more intimidating. In *The Children,* his book about the Nashville group of the Student Nonviolent Coordinating Committee (SNCC), David Halberstam tells how they became silent as the bus from Montgomery crossed the state line with its signs "WELCOME TO MISSISSIPPI THE MAGNOLIA STATE" and "PREPARE TO MEET THY GOD."

Black suffering was not news, and in 1964, after three years of literally being beaten down to the ground, they made the decision to bring in young, white volunteers in the hope that this would draw media attention and protection by the national government. The first group of volunteers was going through orientation on the Oxford, Ohio, campus of Western College for Women. The Mississippi program director, Robert Moses, was speaking when a message was whispered to him. He stood silent for several minutes and then told the volunteers, "Yesterday morning, three of our people left Meridian, Mississippi, to investigate a church-burning in Neshoba County. They haven't come back, and we haven't had any word from them."

Early that spring, a young social worker named Michael ("Mickey") Schwerner and his wife, Rita, arrived in Meridian to run a black community center for the Congress of Racial Equality (CORE). In addition to the perilous nature of trying to open up jobs and the voter rolls, he faced other disadvantages. He was white, a New Yorker, and a Jew. He lived in the black quarter and usually dressed in blue jeans, a sweatshirt, and sneakers. He also had a beard. As respectable Mississippians liked to say after his death, what else could be expected "when someone with a name like Schwerner comes down from New York to stir up things?"

The better people of Mississippi looked down on the hooded knights, but if the Klan was trash, a nigger was a nigger, and the Mississippi way of life was under assault. Out-of-state "mixers," presumptuous blacks, and incautious moderates were likely to be spit on, shot at, beaten, burned, and bombed. According to testimony at his trial, Sam Holloway Bowers, owner of the Laurel, Mississippi, Magnolia Consolidated Realty Company and the Sambo Amusement Company (distributor and servicer of pinball and vending machines) and imperial wizard of Mississippi's White Knights of the Ku Klux Klan, had Schwerner marked for elimination.

When Schwerner was joined at the community center by a young Meridian black man named James Chaney and Andrew Goodman, a white New York college student, they too were included in the White Knights' final solution for Schwerner. On June 21, at the beginning of the "Mississippi Freedom Summer," the three drove out to Neshoba County to view the remains of the black Mount Zion Methodist Church that had been burned by the Klan. As his trial later established, the deputy sheriff from the county seat of Philadelphia, Cecil Price, was tipped off that the civil rights workers were there. He arrested Chaney for speeding and Schwerner and Goodman "for investigation." Holding them in jail long enough to work out the necessary plans, he contacted the exalted cyclops of the Neshoba County Klan, the preacher Edgar Ray Killen. Klansmen from the Neshoba and Lauderdale County Klaverns gathered at the Longhorn Cafe to wait until dark. Deputy Price let the prisoners pay their way out, stopped them again outside of town, and turned them over to his fellow Klansmen. Schwerner, Goodman, and Chaney were shot and their bodies buried in an earthen dam on the land of a local farmer named Olen Burrage.

Parents, civil rights leaders, congressmen, and the press de-

Neshoba County Deputy Sheriff Cecil Price (left) and
Sheriff Homer Rainey (right). 1964.

manded that the national government find the missing men. Although President Lyndon Johnson and his advisers believed that constitutionally and politically they could do nothing to protect the living, the disappearance of the three young Neshoba County civil rights workers, two of them middle-class white northerners, pushed the government into action. The hotly debated SNCC decision to put white bodies on the line was painfully paying off. As with the attack on the freedom riders in Alabama, James Meredith's admission to the University of Mississippi, and the demonstrations in Birmingham, something big enough had happened to gain Washington's attention and force its hand.

Robert Kennedy, who had remained on as attorney general, justified involvement in the search under the 1936 "Lindbergh Law" on the grounds that the kidnappers might have crossed the state line, and President Johnson and his Justice Department aides spent long hours in the Oval Office discussing what the national government could do. To the ire of FBI Director J. Edgar Hoover, a team of Kennedy's Civil Rights Division lawyers had already been down to look into the violence festering in southwestern Mississippi. The division's chief, Assistant Attorney General Burke Marshall, reported that it was "very dangerous." Now, with the rising clamor over the disappearance of the three civil rights workers, President Johnson sent former CIA head Allen Dulles to talk to the governor and state leaders. World War II had gotten Hoover excited about spy catching and espionage, and he looked enviously at Dulles and longingly at the CIA post. Taylor Branch, the historian of *America in the King Years,* speculates that sending Dulles to Mississippi was the president's wake-up call to the FBI head.

"Edgar," Johnson told him, "I want you to put people after the Klan and study it from one county to the next. I want the FBI to have the best intelligence system possible to check on the activities of those people."

Flying into Jackson in *Air Force One* to open the FBI's first state headquarters, Hoover privately warned the state's leaders that Klan violence had to stop. Investigating the Klan became a primary concern for the FBI, which was reluctantly pushed into action by events and by Johnson. Where there had been only fifteen FBI agents in Mississippi, now there were ten times that many, with a tough, experienced inspector, Joseph Sullivan, in charge and an equally able agent, Roy Moore, heading the new Jackson office. "Starting immediately," the orders from Washington directed, "every Ku Klux Klan member in Mississippi is to be contacted by agents for the purpose of developing any information in his possession regarding the whereabouts of the three missing civil rights workers; any information concerning past, present, or future plans of violence on the part of the Klan or others: and an effort should be made to develop each Klan member into an informant or source of information."

The charred remains of the missing men's blue Ford station wagon were found by Indians from the nearby Choctaw reservation. FBI men and sailors from the Meridian Auxiliary Naval Air Station began searching the nearby swamps and rivers while white Mississippians watched, scoffed, joked, and lamented their state's crucifixion by the federal invasion. FBI agents initially made little progress in Neshoba County, where they believed that the sheriff and his deputy had been part of the Klan abduction, but they per-

severed, and word was passed around that the proper piece of information would be worth $30,000. On the forty-fourth day, the FBI moved in heavy equipment and began to dig up the rotting bodies from the center of Olen Burrage's dam. Seth Cagin and Philip Dray, in *We Are Not Afraid: The Story of Goodman, Schwerner, and Chaney and the Civil Rights Campaign for Mississippi,* report that the local comment was not "Who did it?" but "Who told?"

The trial of the accused slayers was not held for three more years. A local grand jury refused to return an indictment. State officials complained that the FBI was holding back information. For their part, the federal representatives were perhaps equally justified in their mistrust of the state officials and the premature exposure of their witnesses. Since the state apparently was not going to try the Klansmen, the federal government brought charges under the old Ku Klux Klan Conspiracy Act of 1870, as it had with the killers of Lemuel Penn in Georgia and Viola Liuzzo in Alabama. Obstructed by the Mississippi-born federal referee and by Federal District

Judge Harold Cox, the government could not get indictments and a trial until 1967.

While the murder investigation continued its slow path, Klan violence mounted, and neither local authorities nor the Justice Department offered protection for civil rights workers. Nevertheless, some 650 mostly white, mostly upper-middle-class college students from the North spent the summer alongside the freedom riders and local people, working in freedom schools, community programs, and voter registration. Almost a hundred years before, during Reconstruction, white middle-class teachers from New England had come to the South to teach in the new black schools and had met with ostracism and violence. Schools and churches had been burned, and teachers, male and female, had been beaten and some murdered. Now, in 1964, in a "second Reconstruction," civil rights workers were shot at, beaten, and jailed. During that summer, there were nearly 1,000 arrests of black and white civil rights workers, eighty beatings, and the burning or bombing of at least sixty-five homes, churches, and other buildings. At least eight people died at the hands of the Klan.

Mississippi had not been much of a Klan state since Reconstruction, not even in the 1920s, but now things were different. The initial organizers came from Louisiana's Original Knights of the Ku Klux Klan, who, by the summer of 1964, numbered 1,000 members in the Florida parishes east of Baton Rouge. In Bogalusa, just across the Pearl River from Mississippi, the Original Knights had launched a reign of terror. When a group of leading citizens—including ministers, the former head of the state bar, and the local newspaper editor and radio station owner—invited former Arkansas Congressman Brooks Hays to speak on improving race relations, Klan threats, boycotts, smashed windows, and gunfire forced a cancellation. In response to a wave of abductions and beatings, the shotgun-carrying Deacons for Defense and Justice was organized in the black community. With everyone going about armed, it took a federal court action to prevent open warfare. In December 1965, a three-judge federal panel in New Orleans enjoined the Original Knights and their "dummy front" Anti-Communist Christian Association from interfering with the civil rights of black citizens. In a familiar story, internal fights over where the money was going split the Original Knights, and Robert Shelton's United Klans was there, as usual, to pick up the pieces.

In the spring of 1964, the Original Knights came into Mississippi and began recruiting among the white factory workers in the old river town of Natchez. Soon there was the usual internal conflict over power and money, and amid charges, countercharges, and banishments, most of the Klansmen went over to Mississippi's own newly organized White Knights. Leading the switch were the Laurel businessman Sam Bowers and E. L. McDaniel, a young Red Ball Express Company worker with a dubious financial history who launched his Natchez Klavern on a campaign of racial beatings and bombings.

Sam Holloway Bowers, the imperial wizard of the new White Knights, was not usual Klan stock. He came from planter class on his mother's side, and his paternal grandfather had been a four-term Mississippi congressman. Bowers was considered a deep thinker in the Klan ranks. After four years in the Navy during World War II, he had a year of college at Tulane and finished almost another one in engineering at Southern California. As a small businessman and with his fascination with guns and explosives, he was more representative of the culture from which the Klans drew members.

Across the Klan world, all the competing Klans shared the same basic ritual, creed, and organizational hierarchies of wizards, dragons, titans, cyclopes, kluds, and such. In half a century, no one had improved on the efforts of the master ritualist, Colonel William J. Simmons, who had brought the Klan back to life on a cold November night in 1915 atop Stone Mountain, Georgia. The ritual that Shelton's United Klans and Bowers's White Knights shared was somewhat simplified and much shortened, however, and the White Knights had an oath of secrecy that provided for no exceptions. The fealty to the U.S. Constitution contained the proviso "as originally written." Membership was restricted to white, gentile, native-born male persons, excluding Papists and Mormons. Like most Mississippians, Klansmen were mainly Baptists and Methodists. The goal was "strict segregation of the races and the control of the social structure in hands of the Christian, Anglo-Saxon white men."

Black voting and the whole civil rights invasion was a "Communist plot" directed by the Jews. Throughout the Klan world, the ideology of the California evangelist Wesley Swift was spreading. As the traveling evangelist Reverend Connie Lynch was preaching it in St. Augustine and elsewhere in the South, Sam Bowers was absorbing the "Christian Identity" message from Swift's tapes and printed sermons. Bowers saw himself as a "warrior priest" and called on white Protestant Christians to join him in the race war that was part of the "cosmic battle" against Satan's blacks and Jews.

Imperial Wizard Bowers was not interested in extending his White Knights beyond the borders of Mississippi and unlike other Klans did not go in for public rallies. Secrecy and discipline were all-important. The White Knights had defined four levels of violence: Number 1 was a cross burning, number 2 a whipping, number 3 a firebombing, and number 4 a killing. Bowers's personal approval was necessary for a number 3 or a number 4, and he took part in the planning of the Schwerner, Chaney, Goodman, and Dahmer killings. With the growing pressure from the FBI and leaks within the Klan, Bowers tightened up secrecy. In the 1967 campaign against the Jewish communities of Jackson and Meridian, only a small group—including Bowers, the bomber Tommy Tarrants, and the pretty schoolteacher Kathy Ainsworth—were in on it.

Crosses blazed across Mississippi. By the fall of 1964, Shelton's United Klans had some seventy-six klaverns in the state and Bowers's White Knights another fifty-two. According to the historian John Dittmer, the prize-winning author of *Local People: The Struggle for Civil Rights in Mississippi*, it had been the most violent summer in Mississippi since Reconstruction. The SNCC, CORE, and their summer volunteers clung desperately to their belief in nonviolence. Police violence ruled the daylight hours, and at night, black farmers and householders kept guard with their shotguns ready. As Imperial Wizard Sam Bowers told his legions, "Ours is a nocturnal organization. We work best at night."

The Klan was initially strongest in the southwestern Mississippi hill country. The mills and railroad machine shops of McComb supplied members for the Klan in Pike County, and the civil rights

Memphis

Oxford

Grenada

MISSISSIPPI

Philadelphia

JACKSON

Meridian

Vicksburg

Natchez

Laurel

McComb

Hattiesburg

Liberty

Bogalusa

BATON ROUGE

LOUISIANA

workers in Amite bitterly commented that there was a department in Washington called "Justice" and a town in Amite County named "Liberty." Testifying before a Senate committee a decade later, Assistant Attorney General John Doar related that by the spring of 1964, even before the Schwerner, Chaney, and Goodman murders, Klan violence had begun to show "alarming proportions." In Pike County, between April 1 and June 30, "three black homes and a barbershop were firebombed; three reporters and two local blacks were beaten. In Adams County a black church was vandalized; two civil rights workers were pursued and shot at; four blacks were whipped; another was seriously wounded by shotgun fire; and a local black man was killed. In Madison County, the Freedom House in Canton was shot at twice and bombed; and a civil rights worker was assaulted. Throughout the state, seven other black churches were damaged or destroyed; eight black homes or stores were bombed or shot into; numerous blacks and civil rights workers were harassed or threatened."

Pike County was primarily United Klans country, and to the east in Jones County, Bowers ran his Sambo Amusement Company out of the Forrest County seat in Laurel, within easy reach of Neshoba County and of Vernon Dahmer's home in Hattiesburg. (Forrest County was named for Nathan Bedford Forrest, Confederate cavalry general and grand wizard of the first Klan.) In many places, policemen joined the Klan—so, too, did Byron De La Beckwith after his second hung jury for the murder of state NAACP director Evers. Beckwith had become disappointed with the conservatism of the Citizens' Councils, and the Klan promised more action. He was a great hit at Klan meetings, and Klansmen crowded around him for his autograph. In 1965, Bowers made him a kleagle, and Beckwith traveled around Mississippi selling fertilizer for the Delta Liquid Plant Food Company and klandom.

Not only were black churches, homes, and businesses being firebombed or dynamited, so too were white newspapers whose editors saw things wrongly. The *Leader-Call* in Laurel and Hazel Brannon Smith's weekly *Northside Reporter* in Jackson were dynamited, and shots were fired through the windows of the Bill Minor's *Capitol Reporter*. As the Klan's attacks accelerated through the summer, particularly targeting the voter registration campaign, it was surprising that there was not a mounting death toll. Smith had been marked for elimination, but she was out of town when her newspaper was bombed and lived to receive a Pulitzer Prize for her journalistic courage. In Greenville, in the Mississippi River delta, although editor Hodding Carter II was not an integrationist, most white Mississippians considered him a radical for being what the civil rights activists called a "fair-play segregationist." Carter commented that "Mississippians are generally polite until they decide to kill you," and he kept a loaded revolver in the drawer of his desk at the *Delta Democrat-Times*.

McComb had been particularly dangerous territory for black people, and Bob Moses and a number of the early SNCC organizers received their first serious Mississippi beatings there. Hodding Carter told the story of a McComb insurance man, "Red" Heffner, who agreed to talk with several of the white volunteers. He had been his company's "Salesman of the Year," his wife was the daughter of the governor's law partner, and their daughter was the winner of the state "Miss Mississippi" pageant. He thought that he was safe and that there was nothing wrong in looking into things. He was wrong. His family was threatened, his dog was poisoned, and his wife and daughter were ostracized by people they had known all their lives. With his business wrecked, "Red" Heffner and his family left McComb and Mississippi.

The Heffners' troubles were dramatic, but the Heffners were white and could start again elsewhere, interestingly working for the Community Relations Service and Headstart in Washington, D.C. Civil rights workers were beaten on the Mississippi streets, and black home owners, businessmen, ministers, educators, and their families, narrowly escaping injury and death from the midnight dynamiters, faced hostile police and indifferent FBI agents who accused them of the crimes from which they suffered.

By the end of the summer, the Klan's bombing campaign in McComb had become an indiscriminate effort to intimidate the black community. It was in the national news. The *New York Times* called it "open warfare" and hinted about federal action. Local business was suffering. Someone in Washington phoned local officials and Mississippi Governor Paul Johnson with the rumor that federal troops were being alerted to impose martial law on Pike County. When the governor told local officials that he was going to beat Washington to it and send in the state National Guard, they asked for two days' delay. For the first time, they began arresting the Klan bombers. As historian John Dittmer tells the story, despite a possible death penalty under Mississippi law, the Klansmen pleaded "guilty" or "no contest," obviously confident that they knew what the local judge would do. He gave them suspended sentences, reasoning that they had been "unduly provoked" by agitators who were of "low morality and unhygienic."

Although the McComb bombing ceased, Klan attacks and police harassment continued until Oliver Emmerich, the editor of the *Enterprise-Journal,* risked his paper and his life to describe what had been happening and call for an end to it. McComb civic and business leaders joined him in a "Statement of Principles," calling for the end of threats and harassment and for equal treatment under the law for all citizens. After a brief, well-publicized celebration of openness, life in McComb reverted to segregation, and a somewhat more cautious Klan remained a feared presence. Nevertheless, Dittmer concludes, the McComb story was a triumph for the local black people who, in the middle of Klan country, had organized themselves and refused to back down in the face of violence.

The growing strength of Bowers's White Knights excited competition. E. L. McDaniel once again jumped ship, this time to become grand dragon of Shelton's United Klans. He and Shelton toured Mississippi in a series of nighttime rallies, giving Klansmen the public excitement that they had missed under the more secretive Bowers. Klaverns were increasingly crossing over from the White Knights to the United Klans, and both Klans planned new violence. The United Klan's method was to have the names and addresses of intended victims drawn from a hat so that no one else would know who was going to do which bombing.

Nevertheless, a reaction was mounting against it, and the aroused concern of state governors and federal agents had become enough to make the Klan jittery. Governor Johnson began sending his special investigators into violence-troubled parts of his state. With a list from J. Edgar Hoover, he had dismissed anyone from the state highway patrol who remained in the Klan. The FBI had identified those who had taken part in the Schwerner, Chaney, and Goodman killings, although it would not be until 1967 that they would face a jury.

· 8 ·

Selma

*B*y the mid-1960s, southern politicians were no longer saying "*Never!*" quite so loudly. The use of force by southern policemen such as Eugene "Bull" Connor in Birmingham and Sheriff Jim Clark in Selma, Alabama, served to advance change rather than contain it. The Ku Klux Klan, which had long been calling for racial war, remained unyielding, but having no greater plan than striking back blindly and forcefully, the Klan became the captive of its enemies.

President Lyndon Johnson told Martin Luther King Jr. that there would be no new civil rights legislation in 1965. Congress had just passed the most important civil rights law since Reconstruction, which opened up public accommodations and promised much more. In the view of much of white America, it was time to relax and let tempers and tensions cool, to follow things up slowly, and to consolidate. Black leaders saw it differently. There were still many more rights that needed protection. The right to vote, which meant a seat at the table where decisions were made, was the key to other rights. Black people were not allowed to vote in many parts of the South. Mississippi and Alabama were the worst. The Department of Justice estimated that only 14 percent of the eligible black voters in Alabama and 6 percent in Mississippi were registered compared to half or more of the whites. Across the South, there were twenty-seven counties where a majority of the people were black but where none of them could vote. The right to vote was the big issue, and this was tied in with the need for greater protection against violence, not only from vigilantes and Klansmen but often from police officers and local juries and judges as well.

For the Civil Rights movement, the choice, as the activists saw it, was between black and white cooperation and black separateness. In 1965, the appeal was to cooperation. Martin Luther King Jr. was its leader. While the young workers of the Student Nonviolent Coordinating Committee (SNCC) in Georgia, Alabama, and Mississippi labored to build grassroots confidence and organization, King appealed to black pride and white conscience. "We must be ready for a season of suffering," he warned. His plan, however, was simpler than his path. He would bring his marchers out into the streets until someone cracked somewhere—in Selma, in the statehouse in Montgomery, in Washington, D.C., or perhaps even in the klaverns of the Klan. If would-be black registrants could not get on the voting books, then they must approach the ballot by way of public demonstrations. "We are going to bring a voting bill into being in the streets of Alabama," King told his people.

There was no Klan in the small but important black-belt city of Selma, birthplace of Birmingham Police Commissioner Eugene "Bull" Connor and of the first Citizens' Council in Alabama. What there was in Selma was Sheriff Jim Clark and his mounted posse, Colonel Al Lingo's state troopers, and SNCC organizer Bernard Lafayette with his wife, Colia. Local officials and white citizens agreed that the blacks must be kept in their place, but for more than two months, beginning in January 1965, black men and women gathered in front of Brown Chapel of the AME Church to march on City Hall—or to wherever else their human petition was most likely to gain attention. Soon there were ten times more black names on the police blotter than on the voting rolls, and the barricade, the billy, and the prod had become standard forms of police response. Martin Luther King Jr. and the Southern Christian Leadership Conference joined the SNCC organizers in Selma in an uneasy partnership, and with them came the national media.

Although more than a month of demonstrations brought headlines and volunteers, there was no sign of a breakthrough, and so James Bevel announced a march on the state capitol in Montgomery. On Sunday, March 7, a flying wedge of police and troopers followed by a mounted posse swept into the marchers at Edmund Pettus Bridge over the Alabama River. With tear gas, whips, clubs, and cattle prods, they routed the petitioners, beating the fallen and pursuing the rest back to Brown Chapel, sending more than a hundred to the hospital. Sheriff Clark, Lingo, and their men had done what Martin Luther King had not been able to do: They had scored a breakthrough for civil rights.

With a promise from the president for a strong voting bill, a protective order from Judge Frank Johnson, and troops and federal marshals, the success of the march to Montgomery was assured. The gathering in front of the state capitol, with Alabama Governor George Wallace watching through binoculars from behind the blinds of his office windows, symbolized the victory the marchers felt was sure to be theirs. The cost of that victory had already been the lives of a black woodcutter and a white Boston clergyman, and there would be one more.

Among the thousands of students, newspapermen, ministers, priests, rabbis, nuns, FBI and Justice Department men, and citizens who poured into Selma after "Bloody Sunday" was a middle-aged mother of five from Detroit: Mrs. Viola Gregg Liuzzo. A member of the transport committee, she was assigned to drive carloads of marchers back to Selma from Montgomery. On her second trip to Montgomery for passengers, she had just crossed Big Swamp Creek in rural Lowndes County, where the demonstrators had spent the third night of their march, when a car swept past her on a curve of U.S. Highway 80. Two shots were fired, and Liuzzo slumped forward as her Oldsmobile swerved off the road into a barbed-wire fence.

Just after noon the next day, President Johnson announced over national radio and television that Klansmen had been arrested for the murder. Describing the Klan as a "hooded society of bigots" disloyal to the United States, he declared war on the "Invisible Empire." He praised Liuzzo's sacrifice and promised to fight the Klan, as his father had done in Texas during the 1920s. Even Governor Wallace felt that things had gone too far. "Life simply should not be that cheap," he commented.

Finding the Klan suspects had not been difficult for the FBI men who had quickly fanned out to check the highway and interview witnesses. The black educator Lemuel Penn had died in the same manner the summer before in northeastern Georgia. Night patrolling had long been a Klan routine, a way to give the boys "a little action," particularly in Alabama, where the Bessemer-to-Birmingham road occasionally came close to becoming a Klan highway. The FBI knew where to look, for this time one of its undercover informants had been in the car with Liuzzo's killers. The Klansmen, all members of the United Klan's Birmingham chapter, were quickly arrested.

As the case moved toward trial, a curious document appeared in the hands of the Alabama police and the Klan. A request from Baker County Sheriff Jim Clark to the Detroit police had produced a badly distorted report on the Liuzzo family. The word now passed around that she was a frumpish, neurotic woman who had abandoned her family to come to Alabama, and the national media picked up the story.

More than a decade later, a Liuzzo family suit under the post-Watergate Freedom of Information Act unlocked something of the byzantine passages of the FBI and the tortured mind of J. Edgar Hoover. At the same time that the FBI was investigating Klan murderers, Hoover was falsely suggesting to President Johnson that Liuzzo was taking drugs and involved in interracial sex in Alabama and that her Teamsters Union husband had Mafia connections. Even after Hoover's death, the FBI sought to cover its trail. It had only reluctantly shared its information on the bombers of Birmingham's 16th Street Baptist Church and Mississippi, and it took the intervention of the American Civil Liberties Union and Michigan Senator Donald Riegle to shake loose a heavily censored copy of Liuzzo's file to her angry sons.

The shooter, Collie Leroy Wilkins, was twice tried for murder in the Alabama courts in 1965. In Wilkins's first trial, his lawyer, the Klan's imperial klonsel, made much of the fact that the FBI informer, Gary Thomas Rowe Jr., was violating a Klan secrecy oath in testifying. Ten members of the jury voted for a manslaughter conviction, but the remaining two explained that they could not believe a man who violated his oath, and the judge had to declare a mistrial.

In the retrial, Alabama Attorney General Richmond Flowers took over the prosecution, and Arthur Hanes, the former mayor of Birmingham, handled the defense. The Alabama Supreme Court refused to allow the prosecution to exclude Citizens' Council members and white supremacists from the second jury, which found Wilkins not guilty. Wilkins was now a celebrity at Klan parades and rallies. In separate incidents in the Selma voting rights campaign, a Unitarian minister, James Reeb, had been beaten to death. An Episcopal seminarian, Jonathan Daniels, and a young black man, Jimmy Lee Jackson, who tried to shield his mother from being beaten by a state trooper, had been shot. In all three cases, the killers went unpunished.

The confrontation in Selma made the headlines in the eastern press, and President Johnson decided to propose a new voting rights law. With television sets simultaneously tuned to catch all three of the networks, the president had watched the coverage of "Bloody Sunday" at the bridge, with growing anger. A week later, he addressed a joint session of Congress, promising a new voting rights law in the name of "the outraged conscience of a nation." As the television cameras focused in on him, he leaned forward and forcefully enunciated the words that had become the anthem of the movement, "We shall . . . overcome!" Republican Minority Leader Everett Dirksen delivered enough Republican votes to end the southern filibuster in the Senate, and on August 6, 1965, President Johnson signed the bill into law. The Voting Rights Act suspended literacy tests, empowered the national government to send registrars to counties where access to the ballot box was denied, and required Justice Department approval of suspected discriminatory changes in voting procedures.

With the Civil Rights movement out in the streets and highways of the South, explosions of Klan violence had helped produce the Public Accommodation Act of 1964 and the 1965 Voting Rights Act. As these laws took effect, the Klan remained a violent guerrilla resistance movement. Its chaotic reaction to the black revolution in the mid-1960s had resulted in at least a dozen murders. Most of them were committed by Mississippi's White Knights, and it was not over yet. In January 1966, five months after the passage of the Voting Rights Act, Sam Bowers's White Knights struck again in Mississippi. Vernon Dahmer, a successful black storekeeper and civic leader in Hattiesburg, was collecting poll tax money to get black voters registered and died when the White Knights firebombed his home.

· 9 ·

Making the Justice System Work

*I*n June 1966, James Meredith, who had entered the University of Mississippi with the aid of the federal judiciary, 500 federal marshals, and the U.S. Army, set out on a solitary march from Memphis to the Mississippi state capitol in Jackson. The purpose of his "walk against fear" was to convince black people that they should not be afraid to vote in the upcoming Democratic primary. As Meredith crossed the state line from Tennessee on U.S. Highway 51, an assassin hiding in the bushes brought him down with a shotgun blast from behind.

While Meredith recuperated in the hospital, black leaders rushed to Mississippi to take his place. It was on that renewed march, in the delta city of Greenwood, that an angry Stokely Carmichael first raised the cry of "black power." Temporarily detouring from the march, Martin Luther King Jr. joined a memorial service for the three murdered Neshoba County civil rights workers. Surrounded by a hostile white crowd that included Deputy Sheriff Cecil Price, King told the mourners, "I believe in my heart that the murderers are somewhere around me at this moment." "You're damn right," Price muttered, "They're right behind you right now" (David Garrow, *Bearing the Cross: Martin Luther King, Jr., and the Southern Christian Leadership Conference*, 483).

It had been two years since the deaths of Michael Schwerner, James Chaney, and Andrew Goodman, but their killers still walked free. Across the South, blacks and civil rights workers were beaten on the streets and in the jails; no law officers stood trial, and local juries set accused Klansmen free. Victims, such as Dr. Hayling in St. Augustine, were charged with assault on their assaulters, and in

67

Mississippi and elsewhere black people whose homes were fire-bombed were often accused of arson. The 1954 U.S. Supreme Court school desegregation decision and the 1964 and 1965 Civil Rights Laws opening up public accommodations and the right to vote contained great potential for change. In the mid-1960s, Klan violence threatened to destroy it in the streets of the Deep South. Local justice systems refused protection, and the U.S. government believed that it did not have the constitutional right to step in. Under the American federal system, most crimes of violence, including murder, fell under state jurisdiction. If the state did not act, Washington could not. That was the governing belief. The crucial battle was to change both federal constitutional theory and state behavior.

Neither seemed very likely. In focusing on voter registration, the young civil rights workers knew where the power lay. As they liked to say, there was more at stake than being able to sit down at a lunch counter and eat a hamburger. When black people were not on the voting rolls, they could not serve on juries or affect the election and actions of sheriffs and judges. As long as the police remained hostile and the court system did not function, the problem of protection remained a life-and-death affair.

In his highly useful history *Federal Law and Southern Order: Racial Violence and Constitutional Conflict in the Post-Brown South,* Michal Belknap writes that "the ultimate security for perpetrators of racist violence was the jury system." Despite FBI evidence that often included signed confessions, local prosecutors did not prosecute, grand juries failed to indict, and trial juries refused to convict Klansmen. Despite confessions obtained by the FBI, prosecutors refused to prosecute the killers of Charles Moore and Henry Dee, whose beaten and dismembered bodies were fished out of a Mississippi River bog. Juries set bombers free in Jacksonville, Atlanta, Birmingham, and Montgomery. They failed to convict the killer of Medgar Evers, Mississippi state leader of the National Association for the Advancement of Colored People; the killer of the white "Freedom Walk" mailman William Moore, who was shot down on the road to Anniston; the killers of the black educator Lemuel Penn, who was gunned down on the highway

outside Athens, Georgia; and the Klansmen who killed Viola Liuzzo on the road between Selma and Montgomery.

If Klansmen, such as the Anniston bus burners and the Mc-
Comb bombers, should happen to get convicted, sympathetic local
judges could be counted on to see that they spent only a short
time—or none at all—in jail. The Klansman who gunned down
Meredith was sentenced to five years in prison, with three suspended. For more serious sentences, in the tradition of Georgia's
earlier governor, Eugene Talmadge, who had set a Klan flogger
free, there was the possibility of a pardon from Arkansas Governor
Orval Faubus or Alabama Governor George Wallace.

Even so, the tide was turning. One important factor in that
change was the Ku Klux Klan itself. The cumulative effect of Klan
violence and the police brutality in Birmingham helped pass the
broad 1964 Civil Rights Act, which forbade discrimination in public accommodations. Again, conflict and police brutality in Selma
and the Klan murder of Viola Liuzzo helped produce the 1965
Voting Rights Act. Many southern politicians became noticeably
more cautious as the number of black voters rose. In Mississippi,
the increasing tempo of Klan bombing and dynamiting alarmed
Governor Paul Johnson and other state leaders who had lost control of a resistance that seemed to be turning into anarchy.

By mid-decade, Washington was finally willing to confront
Klan violence directly where state prosecutors and juries would
not. Both state and national action depended on the FBI. The
breakdown of law and order in Mississippi forced a new activist role
on that reluctant agency. Having pushed the U.S. Supreme Court
to new interpretations of the Reconstruction-era Ku Klux Klan
laws (discussed later in this chapter), the Justice Department's Civil
Rights Division, led by John Doar, brought the killers of Lemuel
Penn and the killers of the three Philadelphia, Mississippi, civil
rights workers into federal court.

The response of the FBI depended on its able but authoritar-
ian, paranoid director, J. Edgar Hoover. Hoover had ruled the bureau with an iron hand since its founding four decades before. With
an eye for publicity and a fierce defensiveness against any challenge,
he had built the FBI into a national icon. He had seen attorneys
general and presidents come and go, and he knew all the Washington

secrets. The Kennedys did not dare to replace him, and Lyndon Johnson kept him on, saying that like a camel allowed into a desert tent, it was better to have Hoover "pissing out" than have him outside "pissing in."

Hoover disliked minorities, the Civil Rights movement, and black leaders, particularly Martin Luther King Jr. He ordered surveillance and was keeping files on the Southern Christian Leadership Conference, the Student Nonviolent Coordinating Committee, the Congress of Racial Equality, and the summer volunteers. The FBI had no black agents and, apart from its bombing investigations, had little experience with racial and civil rights cases. Field agents in the South worked with local police forces and often shared their racial attitudes. Until the disappearance of Schwerner, Chaney, and Goodman, the FBI had little interest, no state headquarters, and few field agents in Mississippi. The Justice Department's Civil Rights Division found FBI reports of so little use for its voting rights cases that it was forced to spell out elaborately detailed instructions and often use its small staff of attorneys to do the basic investigative fieldwork.

Once fully committed, however, the FBI worked hard at investigating Klan violence, but there were continuing problems over the FBI's role and what Hoover would do with the evidence. During the 1961 "freedom rides" in Alabama, the FBI's Birmingham Klan informer, Gary Thomas Rowe Jr., told the FBI of the arrangement between the police and the Klan, but Hoover did not warn the Justice Department. While the "freedom riders" were beaten by the Klansmen, including by Gary Rowe Jr., FBI agents only watched from the sidelines. The FBI did supply evidence for the trial of the Anniston bus burners and gathered the evidence that would eventually send the bombers of Birmingham's 16th Street Baptist Church to die in prison. In the mottled world of racial politics in Alabama, the FBI's careful investigation of the bombing was disrupted when Governor Wallace's public safety director, Al Lingo, jumped in and arrested the chief suspects. Robert Chambliss and two of his coconspirators were given suspended sentences for misdemeanor possession of dynamite. After that, Hoover never told the Justice Department what evidence he had. It was not until after his death in 1972 that the FBI reluctantly helped Alabama's new attorney general, William J. Baxley, to prosecute and convict Chambliss.

In Mississippi, FBI agents now aggressively interviewed all known and suspected Klansmen, keeping them under surveillance, returning again and again for further questions, talking with their wives when they were not home, and conspicuously parking in front of their houses. When a Klansman threatened to shoot any FBI man who set foot on his property, agents walked up to his door and, standing on separate sides of his porch, politely asked him what he intended to do about it.

FBI agents did not themselves infiltrate the Klan. Only rarely did someone from the outside, such as Stetson Kennedy in the late 1940s and investigative *Tennessean* reporter Jerry Thompson in the early 1980s, penetrate the close in-group class world of the klavern, but the FBI successfully developed sources. Across the South, the FBI claimed close to 2,000 informants. Klansmen, always inclined to talk too much about their deeds, found their boasts being used against them. Others recoiled from Klan violence, collapsed under FBI surveillance and questioning, or were enticed by cash payments and promises of lighter sentences. Since the days of the Reconstruction Klan, there has almost always been a Klansman to "tell all" in court. FBI informant Thomas Gary Rowe Jr. was in the murder car from which Viola Liuzzo was gunned down on the highway between Selma and Montgomery. Their consciences troubled by the Neshoba murders, a Meridian police sergeant and a young Baptist minister, high up in Imperial Wizard Sam Bowers's White Knights, became FBI informants and testified when the Klan killers were finally brought to trial.

Initially, the evidence and confessions did not produce convictions and meaningful sentencing. Liuzzo's killer had been found not guilty in Alabama. Despite an experienced prosecutor appointed by the Georgia governor, Colonel Lemuel Penn's killers were acquitted. The Schwerner–Chaney–Goldman accounting was hung up in the intricacies of Mississippi judicial politics and seemed unlikely to come to trial.

At this point, a frustrated Justice Department began what would amount to a major constitutional move. Since murder convictions could not be had in state courts, the Justice Department would now attempt to try Klansmen for violating the civil rights of their victims. Although it involved the same actors and the same victims, it would be a different charge and thus would not legally be double jeopardy, but the question of states' rights still remained. The FBI had already become the investigative arm of both state and national government in cases of racial violence. Under the American system of federalism, what would the U.S. Supreme Court make of the Justice Department and the federal courts becoming the trial courts?

In 1870 and 1871, during Reconstruction, Congress had attempted to control the mounting violence against the newly freed slaves and Republicans. The two Enforcement Acts and a third law, generally known as the Ku Klux Klan Act, were designed to protect the rights of U.S. citizens from private conspiracies or those in which state officials took part. If a policeman or sheriff were involved in the violence, this action, "under color of law," could bring in the national government. These laws were based on the "equal protection" and the "rights of U.S. citizens" clauses of the Fourteenth Amendment (1868) and the "voting rights" clause of the Fifteenth Amendment (1870). The Fourteenth Amendment began with a definition of dual citizenship, both of the state in which a person resided and of the United States. The states were not to violate the rights that came from U.S. citizenship and had to provide equal protection to all citizens. As with other amendments, Congress was authorized to make laws to enforce these rights. In 1875, a Republican-dominated Congress did just that, passing a Civil Rights Act prohibiting both public and private discrimination.

The supremacy of the Union over the states had been determined on the battlefields of the Civil War, but federalism still remained. Democrats opposed, and many Republicans felt uneasy over the expanded powers of the national government. The central constitutional question was, What were the national citizenship rights as protected by the Fourteenth Amendment?

The Supreme Court agreed with the doubters. In a series of landmark cases, which marked the retreat from Reconstruction, the Court rejected the nationalist position. In the *Slaughterhouse Cases* (1873), *U.S. v. Cruikshank* (1876), and *U.S. v. Harris* and the *Civil Rights Cases* (both of 1883), the Court narrowly limited the definition of "national" rights and held that the national government could act only when these rights were violated by state action. When a Louisiana courthouse was burned by a large mob of whites and a hundred black people were killed, the *Cruikshank* Court ruled that the national government could do nothing about it. In the *Civil Rights Cases* ten years later, the Court struck down the 1875 law against discrimination by private individuals. With *Plessy v. Ferguson*'s 1896 acceptance of a "separate but equal" that was never equal, the federal court had all but abandoned the protection of black people and their civil rights.

The gains of the post–World War II Civil Rights movement have obscured much of the fact that civil rights was a very new concern. It was not until well into the twentieth century that the federal judiciary became interested. Beginning with a case under a New York State criminal anarchy law in *Gitlow v. New York* (1923), the Supreme Court began a process of "incorporation," whereby it increasingly applied the Bill of Rights' restrictions on the federal government to the states as well. Conversely, somewhat later and most notably with the 1954 school desegregation decision in *Brown v. Topeka* and the 1964 Public Accommodation Act and the 1965 Voting Rights Act, the federal courts and the national government became increasingly involved in areas that had previously been considered the primary, if not the sole, concern of the states.

The response of the Johnson administration to Klan violence marked a major turning point in the national government's protection of minorities and civil rights workers. It produced Supreme Court decisions, new laws, and successful anti-Klan prosecutions. In the spring of 1966, the Supreme Court handed down crucial decisions in the cases of the Schwerner–Chaney–Goldman murders in Mississippi and the Penn murder in Georgia. In Mississippi, obstruction and dismissal in federal court had kept the case from coming to trial. In Georgia, after the accused had been acquitted in state court, a federal court had denied the jurisdiction of the national Reconstruction-era laws.

The Justice Department appealed, and in unanimous decisions handed down on the same day in March 1966, the Supreme Court agreed with the government's argument. The alleged participation of Deputy Sheriff Price, the Court decided in *U.S. v. Price*, brought the Schwerner–Chaney–Goodman murders under the "state action" provision of the 1870 Enforcement Act. Penn's murder, *U.S. v. Guest* declared, violated his privilege as a U.S. citizen to engage in interstate travel.

Arguing before the Court for the right of the national government to act, Burke Marshall and John Doar had been fearful of the precedent of the twenty-year-old Supreme Court ruling in the 1945 *Screws v. U.S.* decision. Claude Screws, sheriff of Baker County, Georgia, and two deputies had gone to the home of Robert Hall, a young black man, and arrested him for stealing a tire. At the jail, a handcuffed Hall was taken out of the car and beaten to death. In a unique action, the federal government tried Sheriff Screws under the old Reconstruction protection law, and a federal jury found him guilty. Screws appealed on the grounds that the federal government had no jurisdiction. When his appeal reached the Supreme Court, it decided that while the sheriff's action might have come under the government's jurisdiction, the federal trial judge had not properly instructed the jury. Killing the handcuffed prisoner to prevent escape, as the sheriff maintained he had done, did not make it a federal case. Only if the sheriff's action had been a "willful" effort to deprive the prisoner of his constitutional rights could it bring in the federal government. To this, Justices William O. Douglas, Hugo Black, and all but one of the other justices agreed. The case was sent back for retrial, and Sheriff Screws was found not guilty. Faced with the intractable evidentiary problem of proving intent, for two decades the Justice Department brought no further cases under the Reconstruction law. Now, in 1966, what the Supreme Court would do with *Price* and *Guest* could not be predicted.

Times change, minds change, and personnel on the bench changes. In its unanimous March 1966 decisions, the Court ignored the problem of "intent" and reinstated the federal cases. In the *Guest* decision, six of the justices went beyond upholding the federal jurisdiction to try the killers of Penn. In what was taken as an invitation to Congress, they expressed their belief that Congress had the power to punish civil rights violence, whether or not there had been state involvement. President Johnson responded by directing the Justice Department to draft a civil rights protection law.

It was clear that the Supreme Court and the president were resolved to act against anti–civil rights violence.

The proposed protection law, which increased penalties up to life imprisonment where death resulted and extended the reach of the law beyond conspiracies to single violators, was added to an "open housing" bill. A senatorial filibuster and a backlash against "black power" initially kept it from passing. In 1968, the reaction to the murder of Martin Luther King Jr. and the rising tide of ghetto riots made the difference. To please conservative lawmakers, a provision, sometimes known as the "Stokely Carmichael and H. Rap Brown clause," was added, making it a crime to cross a state line to incite a riot. On April 11, 1968, President Johnson signed the Housing Bill, with its civil rights protection and its antiriot clause (U.S. Code, Title 18, Sections 241, 242, and 245), into law.

· 10 ·

Klansmen on Trial & the Klan's Campaign of Terror against the Jews of Mississippi

The Department of Justice did not intend to let the murder of Viola Liuzzo rest. In December 1965, Klansman Collie Leroy Wilkins, having been acquitted in the state courts of Alabama, now faced Assistant Attorney General John Doar in Judge Frank Johnson's federal court. The Supreme Court's *Guest* decision was still three months off, and there was question over just what rights came under federal jurisdiction. The government argued that Mrs. Viola Liuzzo was covered by Judge Johnson's order protecting the Selma-to-Montgomery march. Judge Johnson, presiding over the trial, agreed.

With the departure of Burke Marshall, Doar had become the head of the Justice Department's Civil Rights Division. He was a northerner, arguing his cases before southern juries. With the trial held in federal court in Montgomery, Doar had an upper-middle-class jury, unlike the farmers and small-town jurors who had served in state court. The legal historian Michal Belknap pointed out that although the charge was the conspiracy, Doar handled it as a murder. Unlike Baxter's attack on racism that had resulted in the state court acquittal, Doar presented the case as a law-and-order question. None of the defendants took the stand, and defense appeals to prejudice and attacks on the informer Gary Rowe were ineffectual. The jury found Wilkins and other Klansmen guilty, and the federal appeals court upheld the verdict. Since the case under federal law was for conspiracy to deny civil rights, not for murder, the maximum legal punishment was ten years in prison, and Judge Johnson gave it to them.

Doar, a Republican, had originally been appointed by President Dwight Eisenhower. Kept on by the Kennedys and Lyndon Johnson, he became the point man in the Justice Department's voting rights cases. Finding that the FBI was not producing the necessary investigative information, he had gone in person to interview evicted sharecroppers in Tennessee's Haywood County and had traveled the back roads of Mississippi gathering evidence on voter discrimination. In another decade, he would be the counsel for the House Judiciary Committee's impeachment investigation of President Richard Nixon. He had reported to Attorney General Robert Kennedy on the beating of the "freedom riders" in Montgomery, helped bring James Meredith on campus at the University of Mississippi, negotiated between Martin Luther King Jr. and the businessmen of Birmingham, and stood in the middle of the street between angry black protestors and the heavily armed police in Jackson, Mississippi, after the funeral of Medgar Evers.

With the Supreme Court now having upheld federal jurisdiction in the *Guest* decision, the Justice Department moved on to Georgia. The killers of Lemuel Penn had been acquitted in state court, but the government again prevailed on the federal charges. Penn's killers were found guilty of violating his civil rights and, like Liuzzo's murderer, received the maximum ten-year sentence.

Now it was Mississippi's turn, and Doar again headed up the federal prosecution. In reality, the trial and the ultimate conviction, which neither Mississippi nor a national audience expected, were probably made possible only by the delay. In 1964, it was not likely that a Mississippi judge and jury would have produced a guilty verdict. By 1967, the federal case had been tightened against procedural error, and local feeling was changing. The all-white, working-class federal jury, drawn from a larger and integrated district panel, listened soberly and attentively to confessions of three Klan participants and to Doar's low-key presentation of the evidence. The defense offered character and alibi witnesses. None of the defendants took the stand.

Doar summed up for the prosecution, giving the jury reason to separate themselves from Klan lawlessness:

This crime was not the act of any loyal citizen of Mississippi. . . . This was no representative group of the State of Mississippi; but this was a small, secret, militant group, masterminded by a fanatic who singled out Schwerner as a man who had to be eliminated. Not to preserve or protect Mississippi, but rather to satisfy his own consuming hatred. . . . If you find these men . . . not guilty of this conspiracy, it would be true to say that there was no night-time release from jail by Cecil Price; there were no White Knights; there are no young men dead; there was no murder. If you find that these men are not guilty, you will declare the law of Neshoba County to be the law of the State of Mississippi.

The defense denounced the prosecution's "paid witnesses" and attacked the victims who had "violated the American constitution by messing in local affairs in a local community." "Mississippians rightfully resent some hairy beatnik from another state visiting our state with hate and defying our people," the Klansmen's lawyer argued.

When the jury initially reported itself deadlocked, Judge Harold Cox sent them back again, telling the dissenters that although they ought not to yield their own convictions, they should give favorable consideration to the position of the majority. Lawyers and reporters call this the "dynamite charge," and Judge Johnson had used it to bring a verdict in the Liuzzo trial. When the jury convened the next morning, it quickly brought in a verdict. Klan Wizard Sam Bowers, Neshoba Deputy Sheriff Cecil Price, and five other Klansmen were pronounced guilty. Klansmen who had not been identified as present at the killing were either acquitted or, like Neshoba Klavern leader preacher Edgar Ray Killen, escaped when the jury could not agree on a verdict. Price and another Klansman, who had commented within earshot of the judge that they might give the jury a "dynamite charge" of their own, were denied bail while the judge considered the sentencing.

Because Price had taken part in the murders, this made the Klansmen part of a conspiracy "under the color of law" and brought the killing under the old Reconstruction-era Enforcement Acts. As a result, the Klansmen were convicted not of murdering Schwerner, Chaney, and Goodman but of violating their civil rights. Judge Cox sentenced Bowers to the maximum ten years, Price to six, and the others to three. In 1970, with all appeals exhausted, the men entered federal prison, where Price served four years and Bowers six.

For Bowers, there were still more indictments to face. In the summer of 1965, Robert Shelton had mounted a major campaign to take control of Mississippi Klandom from Bowers. Crowds of 1,000 and more turned out for his United Klan rallies across the state from Natchez to Meridian, and Shelton claimed switch-overs of whole klaverns of former White Knights. Neshoba Sheriff Lawrence Rainey and his deputy, Price, disappointed over Bowers's failure to raise more defense money, were among the United Klans' conspicuous new recruits.

Pushed by the competitive pressure, the White Knights stepped up their harassment, cross burning, nocturnal shotgun blasts, arson, and bombing in the Laurel–Hattiesburg area. Bowers was particularly angry over Vernon Dahmer's voter registration campaign and impatiently ordered a number 3 and a number 4 on the black storekeeper.

After Bowers had rehearsed his hit team in a nearby graveyard, they made several drive-by reconnnaissances and then struck after midnight. Two carloads of Klansmen set Dahmer's store and home on fire with gasoline bombs and fired into the house with pistols and shotguns. Dahmer, awakened from sleep in the back of the house, picked up his shotgun and stood firing through the flames while his wife and three children, four sons being away in the service, escaped out the back. Dahmer's lungs were seared by the flames, and he died in the hospital the next day.

FBI agents hurried over from Jackson, set up headquarters in Hattiesburg's Holiday Inn, and began their investigation. There was much to go on at the crime scene. There were plastic gasoline containers, ejected shells, a dropped pistol, and, a short distance away, one of the Klan cars, a blue Ford, which had been mistakenly shot up by Klansmen from the other car. Local opinion was outraged by the killing, and the county sheriff and state police helped with the investigation. A wealthy farmer and oil-well owner who had been one of Bowers's first recruits and financial contributors agreed to help persuade other participants to confess. The FBI soon had a list of suspects, all members of Laurel Klan No. 4. One of the shooters, who had driven the other attack car, was a successful businessman with four young children, a PTA and Boy Scout leader, and president of the Laurel Jaycees. His selection as "Jaycee of the Year" was followed shortly by his indictment for the murder. Eventually, in 1968, a local jury convicted four of the Klansmen. The Jaycee and two others went to Parchman prison on life sentences, but in a year he was home again on various leaves and work release. By the end of the 1970s, all the Klansmen were out of prison.

When the Dahmer killing first came to trial in 1968, Imperial Wizard Bowers was free on appeal of his 1967 conspiracy conviction for the Neshoba murders, and there had been two more Klan killings—a black farmer and the treasurer of the National Association for the Advancement of Colored People in Natchez—and a bombing campaign against the Jewish communities of Jackson and Meridian. Bowers was the planner; others carried out the attacks. Repeatedly brought to trial on various charges in Dahmer's death, Bowers escaped through a mistrial and three hung juries. Local sentiment was turning against him. The vote in his first trial for arson was eleven to one for conviction. In his second trial, this time for murder, it was ten to two. Unconvicted and unshaken, Bowers was angry at what he saw as the "Jew–Communist" plot against the white people of Mississippi. His reign of terror was not yet over.

As Klan membership collapsed under FBI pressure, informers, and indictments, Bowers's belief in the importance of secrecy was forcefully confirmed. His rancor against the Jews, whom he believed were behind the civil rights revolution, grew. The Neshoba trial, which had resulted in the conviction of Bowers and six other Klansmen for violating Schwerner, Chaney, and Goodman's civil rights, had taken place in Meridian. While the appeal process went on, a rash of Klan bombings seemed intended to punish the community for such impiety, and Bowers's campaign against the Jews of Mississippi accelerated.

There were 1,000, mostly old, established Jewish families in Mississippi. They lived in the cities, such as Jackson and Meridian, making their living mainly in commerce and the professions. Jewish

Mississippians had fought on the southern side in the Civil War and often shared the racial attitudes of other white Mississippians. Mississippians were a friendly people except where matters of honor and race were concerned. Although Jews were not invited to be members of the country club, they fit in. Jewish Mississippians had no intention of causing disturbance, but times were changing, and so were the internal pressures within the Jewish communities. The Civil Rights movement added to the pressures, not the least being that a significant number of the summer volunteers were Jewish.

In her book *The Temple Bombing,* Melissa Fay Green told of how a new rabbi from the North challenged the passive assimilationist culture and segregationist values of Atlanta's German Jewish community. Jack Nelson, the *Los Angeles Times'* prime southern reporter, told a similar story in his account of the Klan's campaign against the Jews of Mississippi, *Terror in the Night: The Klan's Campaign against the Jews.* Like Rabbi Jacob Rothschild in Atlanta, Rabbi Perry Nussbaum emphasized the distinctiveness of Jewish religion and life, and, to the alarm of many in Jackson's Temple Beth Israel congregation, Nussbaum reached out to Mississippi's small but growing interracial Civil Rights movement. He took a lead in the Committee of Concern's fund-raising to rebuild black churches and brought meetings of the racially mixed Mississippi Council on Human Relations into the newly dedicated Beth Israel.

In September 1967, a month before the trial of the Neshoba Klansmen was scheduled to begin in Meridian, a dynamite bomb wrecked Jackson's Temple Beth Israel. This was followed by the bombing of the homes of black and white civil rights leaders, including Rabbi Nussbaum's. Five black churches were burned in Meridian, and in May 1968 a powerful explosion wrecked Meridian's Beth Israel synagogue. The bombing of the Jackson synagogue had produced condemnation from many but not all of the Christian pulpits, the leading Baptists being among the silent. Governor Johnson, who had said nothing about the burning of black churches, denounced the synagogue bombing as "almost unthinkable . . . in this civilized state among our civilized people."

Pushed by Mississippi Senator James Eastland, J. Edgar Hoover poured resources into the hunt for the bombers, but FBI informers and renewed pressure on Klan suspects produced no results. Having been brought to court in both the Neshoba and the Dahmer trials through the testimony of informers, Bowers had painful justification for his belief in secrecy. With a small inner group now carrying on the new bombing campaign, he had reason to believe that he was safe from the FBI's informants. Central to his campaign were his bomb maker, a well-to-do electrical contractor, and the twenty-one-year-old Thomas Albert Tarrants III. Tarrants had grown up in Mobile, Alabama, with an angry segregationist father and a love of guns. He had hung out with the fiercely anti-Semitic National States Rights Party and Minuteman people. Like Bowers, he had listened to the tapes of the Church of Jesus Christ Christian's Wesley J. Swift, who preached the early Christian Identity anti-Semitic gospel. Now, in the summer of 1967, Tarrants came to Laurel to meet Bowers and became his bomber. He kept his distance from the Klan and its hangouts, where the FBI was looking for the bomber.

On July 1, 1968, the headline on Jack Nelson's page 1 story in the *Los Angeles Times* read, "*Mississippi Police Thwart Dynamiting: One Dead, One Wounded.*" A police and FBI stakeout at the home of a Jewish businessman in Meridian had captured Tarrants, who, though badly wounded, had fought back with pistol and submachine gun and had almost escaped. His armed companion in the car, an attractive, young fifth-grade Jackson schoolteacher named Kathy Ainsworth, died in the hail of bullets. While her new husband was away in National Guard camp, she had become Tarrants's nocturnal accomplice. She had grown up in Florida with a mother who vented her hatred of Jews and gone to school at Mississippi College, where her prejudices were fueled by an arch-segregationist professor and the Wesley Swift tapes of her roommate's father. She teamed up with Tarrants, whom she had met in Mobile, and joined the Klan and Americans for the Preservation of the White Race. During the day, she was the friendly fifth-grade teacher; at night, she learned weapons and bomb making. Wearing a tight, low-cut blouse and high-cut shorts, she rode with Tarrants. Now she was dead, and Tarrants was in prison.

Two years later, Nelson had a new headline in the *Los Angeles Times:* "*Police Arrange Trap: Klan Terror Is the Target.*" The troubled head of Mississippi's Council on Human Relations had given him the lead, and Nelson had returned to Mississippi and traced down the rest of the story. The FBI and the Meridian sheriff, who had cleaned Klan influence out of his department, had decided that the only way to stop the wave of terror was to lure the Klan bombers into ambush. With enough pressure and money, they believed that they could get insiders to help set up the unknown bombers. Their own names were already on the Klan hit list, and now they brought in the regional director of the Jewish Anti-Defamation League (ADL) to listen to a tape of Klansmen plotting to blow up synagogues during services. A total of forty-five thousand dollars was secretly raised, and the FBI and the Meridian police began the torturous secret negotiations for the delivery of the unknown bombers.

All this was set forth in Nelson's story and in his book *Terror in the Night*. The informants were the Roberts brothers: Alton Wayne Roberts, who had shot civil rights workers Mickey Schwerner and Andrew Goodman, and his brother Raymond. Out on appeal from the conviction in the Neshoba killing, Alton Wayne had the trust of Tarrants and his fellow bomber. They agreed that the bombing target would be a Jewish Meridian businessman, Meyer Davidson, who had been outspoken against the Klan. The FBI secretly evacuated Davidson and his family. With the agents and an army demolition team standing by, dark-clad police officers from the Meridian sheriff's special squad staked out the area around Davidson's house. Nothing happened the first night. On the second night, they took their positions once again. Raymond Roberts managed to phone the police that the second hit man, Danny Joe Hawkins, was fearful that he was being watched by the FBI and would not be on this assignment. A woman wearing shorts had replaced Hawkins, but Roberts did not know who she was.

As Tarrants approached the Davidson house carrying the bomb, a detective called out for him to stop. He dropped the bomb and fired. The police opened up with rifles and shotguns, and Kathy Ainsworth died as she reached across the front seat to help Tarrants back into the car. Although wounded, Tarrants got the car going and escaped a roadblock by cutting across a lawn. Rammed by a police car, he jumped out firing his submachine gun, wounding an officer and killing an unlucky civilian. He was finally brought to the ground by an electrified fence and bullets and shotgun pellets. By now, a crowd of neighbors had gathered, and the police could not carry out the final step in their ambush.

J. Edgar Hoover was furious over the second story detailing the planning of the ambush execution and denied that the FBI had played any part in it. Placing Nelson at the top of his "enemies list," Hoover denounced him as a "drunk" and ordered the FBI to cease all contact with *Los Angeles Times* reporters.

Meridian surgeons saved Tarrants's life and stitched him back together. Recaptured after a jailbreak, Tarrants initially plunged deeper into Klan and Nazi literature before turning to the Bible and serious philosophy. This, in time, led to a religious conversion. Both the Baptist minister who had first told Nelson about the entrapment story and the FBI agent who had arranged it visited Tarrants regularly and believed that he was sincere. Though he refused to testify about the Klan and his fellow bombers, they worked for his early release and brought Al Binder, the lawyer who had organized the fund-raising for his ambush, to see him.

An informant working for both Binder and the FBI brought news that the Klan was plotting the murder of the New Orleans ADL director. The hit man was to be Byron De La Beckwith, the ambush killer of Medgar Evers. A close watch was kept on Beckwith, and when the informant reported that Beckwith was on his way, word was passed to the New Orleans FBI and Police Department. A trap was set, and just after midnight, the New Orleans police stopped Beckwith at a roadblock on an isolated stretch of road outside the city. In his car, they found a revolver, several rifles, parts of a .50-caliber machine gun, a map marked with the route to the ADL director's house, and the large, ticking dynamite bomb. Beckwith served three years in Louisiana's Angola state prison.

Tarrants ingratiated himself with the Parchman staff, who found his intelligence useful and believed that his was no contrived "jailhouse conversion." His friends, the warden, and eventually Binder, who had come to believe that Tarrants had truly changed, supported his application for early release. He was accepted for college by Duke, Rutgers, Earlham, and the University of Mississippi. In 1976, after eight years in prison, without Tarrants having given testimony about the Klan, the governor signed his release. He was an "A" student at the University of Mississippi, concentrating in Greek and the New Testament. He spoke at the governor's annual prayer breakfast and published a book on his prison life and religious conversion. Testifying that his racism and anti-Semitism had long since been washed out by Christian love, Tarrants left Mississippi to marry, raise a family, and teach at a training school for missionaries where Jack Nelson interviewed him for the book on the Klan's war against the Jews of Mississippi.

As Tarrants walked out of Parchman prison in 1976, the Klan's power and organization in Mississippi had long since disappeared. In the same year, the last of the Neshoba killers, Imperial Wizard Bowers, was released from federal prison. Under his rule, according to the FBI's count, the White Knights of the Ku Klux Klan had been responsible for nine murders and at least 300 beatings, burnings, and bombings. Bowers had served six of his ten-year federal sentence for violating the civil rights of Michael Schwerner, James Chaney, and Andrew Goodman. No one had yet been tried under the laws of Mississippi for their murder. In the murder of Vernon Dahmer, Bowers, thanks to the deadlocked juries, still walked free. Without the testimony of Bowers or Tarrants, the bomb maker and the other hit man in the war against the Jews of Mississippi were never arrested.

Byron De La Beckwith had been tried twice in 1964 for the murder of Medgar Evers. Both all-male, white juries deadlocked at ten to two for conviction, and Beckwith also remained free. In Birmingham, the bombing of the 16th Street Baptist Church, in which the four young girls had been killed, was still listed as unsolved.

· 11 ·

Decline

*M*ississippi had been the most resolutely white supremacist and racially repressive of the southern states, home of the Citizens' Councils and the State Sovereignty Commission, most unwilling to recognize the rights of its black citizens. Professor Jim Silver, who left the University of Mississippi under pressure after having chaired the history department and taught there for nineteen years, described Mississippi as a "closed society" in which a silent ministry and a controlled educational system, media, and public life did not permit discussion and differing points of view to be expressed. The official State Sovereignty Commission spied and kept files on Mississippians and helped fund the Citizens' Councils. The councils, first organized in Indianola, Mississippi, after the Supreme Court school decision in 1954, spread across the South, trumpeting white supremacy and segregation and pressuring those who disagreed.

Jackson's family-owned *Clarion-Ledger* and the *Daily News* were the only newspapers with statewide distribution, and they took a hard line in their headlines, news coverage, and editorials. When Byron De La Beckwith, who had been five years old when his mother brought him back to Mississippi, was arrested by the FBI, the *Clarion-Ledger* headlined it "*Californian Is Charged with Murder of Medgar Evers.*" Jackson's NBC and CBS affiliates censored network programming, and national magazines were generally not available. Even a "fair-play segregationist" such as Hodding Carter II was seen as a dangerous radical.

Mississippians were encouraged by their political and cultural leadership to believe that they were facing an oppressive national government and an invasion of race mixers, probably Communist directed. This did not mean that they necessarily liked the Klan, but it was usually safer to be silent. Testifying before a U.S. Senate Committee a decade later, former U.S. Attorney General Nicholas Katzenbach summed up the "unique difficulty" in Mississippi and parts of Alabama and Louisiana of "gathering information on fundamentally lawless activities which have the sanction of local law enforcement agencies, political officials and a substantial segment of the white population."

The murders of Evers, Viola Liuzzo, and other Klan victims were initially helpful to the Klan, which drew its membership almost exclusively from that resentful portion of society that looked on physical resistance as the necessary and suitable expression of beleaguered white manhood. Violence swelled Klan ranks. There was also a wider pool of supporters who saw the Klan as the only organization that did anything to counter the black push into their lives. Even as late as 1967, Evers's assassin, Beckwith, although coming in last in a field of six when he ran for lieutenant governor, drew 34,675 votes. Yet despite initial increase in membership, stirrings of growth and power were merely illusionary.

By the mid-1960s, times were changing, even in Mississippi. School desegregation and the new 1964 Public Accommodation Act were being minimally observed, and the 1965 Voting Rights Act was changing the electorate across the Deep South. Although black people made up a larger portion of the population than in any other state, Mississippi had had the smallest percentage of black voters. By 1970, the eligible black voters who were registered had increased from less than 7 percent to 60 percent. Despite manipulation of voting districts and at-large elections and the impact of deep racial poverty, politics would never be the same. President Lyndon Johnson's young aide, Bill Moyers, told the historian David Halberstam of a conversation with Johnson the night that the Voting Rights Act was approved by Congress. Moyers was surprised to find the president depressed. "I think we've just handed the South over to the Republican party for the rest of our lives," Johnson told him. By the end of the century, Mississippi would have the largest number of elected black officeholders and two white Republican senators, one of them the majority leader in the

U.S. Senate. A Mississippian had been chairman of the Republican National Committee, and in presidential elections, Mississippi proved to be the safest state for Republican candidates.

This would have been difficult for most people to foresee in the mid-1960s. Klan violence had become too reckless to be ignored. The political leadership believed that Mississippi faced a collapse into anarchy and possible intervention by federal troops. This is what had happened in Arkansas at Little Rock's Central High School and at the University of Mississippi. As reckless as Alabama Governors John Patterson and George Wallace might be, they knew when to draw back, and Mississippi's Paul Johnson was no bumbling Ross Barnett. Having removed Klansmen from the state highway patrol, Johnson was quietly cooperating with the Justice Department.

When the Public Accommodation Act was passed, it was not the state politicians but rather the business community that, however reluctantly, led the acceptance. A useful study edited by Elizabeth Jacoway and David Colburn, *Southern Businessmen and Desegregation,* shows the role that business considerations played in fourteen major southern cities. While many politicians called for resistance, businessmen read the costs of social disruption and the boycott of downtown stores, the loss of new industry, and the possible cutoff of federal aid.

Governors Burt Combs of Kentucky and Fritz Hollings of South Carolina helped their states adapt. Governors Harry Byrd of Virginia and Jimmy Davis of Louisiana resisted but did not get their states in as much trouble as Arkansas' Orval Faubus, Mississippi's Ross Barnett, and Alabama's John Patterson and George Wallace. State legislators, city commissions, and aldermen echoed the Citizens' Council's line, but Mayors William Hartsfeld and Ivan Allen Jr. helped keep the peace in Atlanta, and Lester Bates led Columbia, South Carolina, in winning *Look*'s "All-American City" award in 1964. Most mayors followed a rear-guard action and hoped that rioting would not break out in their cities.

In southern cities, power was held by the business and civic elites—owners, managers, bankers, lawyers, and doctors—who had little desire to end segregation. They belonged to the Citizens' Councils and hoped that the trouble would go away. Each city had its own story of success or failure. In some cities, such as Tampa, Dallas, and Columbia, there were biracial committees, and civic leaders guided the changes. In St. Augustine, the motel owners and small businessmen were willing to accommodate if the power structure would give them cover, but the leading banker declined, and the John Birch–minded doctors and lawyers vowed to resist.

In city after city, faced with school closings, loss of business and economic development, civil rights demonstrations, and Klan violence, elites and business communities belatedly became involved. Merchants' associations, committees to open or keep open the schools, councils of 100, chambers of commerce, and other business-oriented groups helped negotiate the end of public discrimination and the quieting of the streets. The board of the Jackson Chamber of Commerce, with an assist from the Roman Catholic bishop, called for compliance with the new 1964 Civil Rights Act, and a Mississippians for Public Education committee was organized. With support from business groups across the state, the Mississippi Economic Council called for lawful acceptance.

In McComb, *Enterprise-Journal* editor Oliver Emmerich had rallied business and civic leaders to take a stand against Klan violence. Now in the fall of 1965, in Sam Bowers's own hometown of Laurel, after a year of Klan terrorism, the newly elected mayor, William Henry Bucklew, stepped forward. Mayor Bucklew was not one of the white moderates who were beginning to raise their heads. He had been a three-state director of George Wallace's 1964 presidential campaign and on the Speakers Bureau of the Mississippi State Sovereignty Commission. Combining both Klansmen and integrationists in his denunciation of "the flood of scum, degenerates, free-lovers, night riders, church burners, home bombers and hooded thugs running loose," he gathered the county's sheriff, police chiefs, and prosecuting attorneys to sign a statement condemning the Klan. The *Laurel Leader-Call* published their statement on its front page along with a listing of the dates, places, and victims of thirty-five acts of Klan terrorism.

Going on local television, Mayor Bucklew explained that he believed in segregation but was tired of fighting the Civil War and was now speaking out—out of shame—for all those who, like himself, had preferred to remained silent. "Many of these fanatics," he said, "talk so much about God. Can you imagine a loving, merciful, forgiving God blessing the act of any creep who would burn a home or a place of worship." He called on the people of Laurel to sign petitions supporting the right of everyone, of whatever race, color, or creed, to be free from violence or harassment. The Jones County Baptist Association passed a resolution of support, and civic spokesmen pointed out the damage of Klan terrorism to economic development. Klan leaders demanded equal time. They went on television to deny that they were involved in violence, and people were anonymously warned not to sign antiterrorist petitions being circulated by the churches. When the *Leader-Call* published the names of some 500 signers, the list included bankers and the representatives of Masonite, which was Laurel's major employer. Although Klan terrorism eased in Laurel, the rage in the heart of Laurel businessman and Imperial Wizard Bowers still burned, and the assault on the life of Vernon Dahmer and on the Jews of Mississippi lay ahead.

Governor Johnson sent Mayor Bucklew a letter of praise, but he and other Mississippi elites, such as Harold Cox, federal judge for Mississippi's southern district, were not racial moderates. Governor Johnson's idea of political humor had been to identify the initials of the National Association for the Advancement of Colored People (NAACP) as standing for "Niggers, Apes, Alligators, Coons, and Possums." Cox had gotten his appointment to his federal judgeship through the power of his college roommate, Mississippi's senior senator, James Eastland, who chaired the Senate Judiciary Committee. President John F. Kennedy had wanted to appoint the top NAACP lawyer, Thurgood Marshall, to the U.S. Court of Appeals, and that meant going through Eastland's Senate Judiciary Committee. "Give me Cox," Eastland told the president, "and you can have the nigger." As judge, Cox treated civil rights workers and black people with contempt—"chimpanzees," he called them—and he had obstructed the government's initial efforts to try the Neshoba murders.

By the time they finally did come to trial, however, Cox presided with stern control. On the first day of testimony, Neshoba Klavern leader and preacher Edgar Ray Killen had his lawyer ask a witness whether young blacks had signed promises to rape white women. Judge Cox demanded to know the source of the question, warning, "I am not going to allow a farce to be made from this trial, and everybody might as well get that through their heads, including every one of the defendants, right now."

Governor Johnson denounced the killers of Vernon Dahmer as "vicious and morally bankrupt criminals." Increasingly, sheriffs and local policemen were willing to help the FBI, which held out the prize of a prestigious training course at FBI headquarters in Washington, D.C. It was not that they had given up their racial beliefs to protect civil rights workers; rather, the Klan was now an outcast. It was no longer seen as an upholder of the cause but an embarrassment and a civil disrupter and danger. With the arrest of Klansmen for the Neshoba and Dahmer murders and Imperial Wizard Bowers being charged in both cases, fear and distrust swept through the klaverns. There was the usual conflict over where the money went and who was going to pay for the lawyers and trial expenses. E. L. McDonald was again having trouble over his handling of Klan finances. In the summer of 1966, Imperial Wizard Robert Shelton expelled McDonald from the United Klans and decided that what was left of his Mississippi realm would have to be run from his own office back in Tuscaloosa, Alabama.

The key elements in the Penn, Liuzzo, and Neshoba convictions were a growing southern feeling against the Klan and its violence, combined with testimony from informers, confessions, and forceful efforts by the federal government. With the state leadership more outspoken, the FBI digging up the facts, and the Justice Department's lawyers presenting them in court, the hooded knights complained that they were being terrorized. Juries had been integrated, and broader jury selection was under way. Federal juries, still southern but taken from larger, regional pools, were more likely to convict for racial violence. The expanded federal civil rights protection law was not passed until 1968, and most cases of violence were still in the hands of state courts, where convictions were possible but sentences seldom fully served.

During the winter of 1965–1966, the Klan had further bad luck, this time in the form of the House Un-American Activities Committee (HUAC). After the murder of Viola Liuzzo on the Selma-to-Montgomery highway, President Johnson called for a congressional investigation of the Klan. The more liberal Justice Committee did not want to touch it, so the HUAC stepped in. It seemed ironic for this committee, whose primary concern had been making accusations about Communist influence in America, to be investigating the Ku Klux Klan, which believed that integration and the Civil Rights movement were a Communist conspiracy. To the surprise of the liberal media and congressmen, who distrusted all HUAC investigations, the subcommittee resolutely dug into the Klan.

Between October 1965 and February 1966, with information supplied by the FBI, a HUAC subcommittee questioned 187 witnesses, including Robert Shelton, Samuel Bowers Jr., J. B. Stoner, Byron De La Beckwith, and a roster of grand dragons and other Klan officials. Led by Louisiana Congressman Edwin Willis and Charles Weltner, a young liberal from Atlanta, the subcommittee produced the best report on the Klan ever to come out of Congress.

Although all but a few of the subpoenaed witnesses used the Fifth Amendment and various other amendments to avoid answering questions, the committee staff produced a report that told much about the fifteen competing Klans and their 714 klaverns. It listed the klaverns, their locations, their names, cover names and fronts, and officers and reported on their meetings, arsenals, and special violent "action" groups. It identified the top state Klan leaders and reported on their educational shortcomings, their criminal records, and how they helped themselves to their members' dues and contributions.

When first subpoenaed, United Klans Imperial Wizard Robert Shelton told the press, "I'll be there with my boots on," but before the committee he appealed to his rights under the Fifth, First, Fourth, and Fourteenth Amendments to refuse to answer questions and turn over Klan records. Under the Constitution, he was within his rights not to answer questions, but Klan records had no such protection. After the full House of Representatives cited him for contempt and the courts upheld it, Imperial Wizard Shelton went off to a year in federal prison.

At their peak in 1964, Bowers's White Knights and Shelton's United Klans had each numbered approximately 6,000 members in Mississippi. By the beginning of 1967, the HUAC estimated the White Knights to be down to 400 members and the United Klans' Mississippi contingent at no more than 750. All together, Shelton's United Klans counted 15,000 members in seventeen states, but the FBI privately claimed nearly 2,000 of them as sources and informants. In Mississippi the Klan world was crumbling, although Bowers's remaining fragment was still particularly deadly.

Throughout the South, there was a growing opposition to the Klan. Only a limited number of communities, whether through fear or approval, countenanced its night riding. In others, law was enforced, and distaste for the Klan was openly expressed. The mayor and local businessmen of Hemingway, South Carolina, protested that Klan rallies nearby gave the false impression that the town approved of the hooded knights. High school students erected signs along the highway with slogans such as "Stamp out Boll Weevils, Tobacco Worms, and the KKK." When the house of a North Carolina black leader was burned down, his fellow townspeople, white and black, contributed money and labor to rebuild it. In Anniston, Alabama, civic and business leaders signed a letter to the newspapers announcing that the Klan was not wanted in their community, and the $20,000 reward they offered led to solution and conviction in a local racial murder.

During the early 1960s, Klansmen met the Civil Rights movement head-on in the city streets of Alabama and the towns and country roads of Mississippi. The outcome hung perilously in the balance. By mid-decade, the Klans seemed no more effective a resistance force than had been the politicians, Citizens' Councils, and the police, sheriffs and their deputies.

In important part, the Klan onslaught had pushed the national government into action, and the southern states were beginning to follow suit. Responding to the leadership of Presidents Kennedy and Johnson, Congress passed the 1964 Public Accommodation Act, the 1965 Voting Rights Act, and the 1968 Housing and Protection Act. The FBI, both within and outside the law, was putting pressure on the Klans, and juries were bringing in guilty verdicts. Black voting blocs were beginning to elect black councilmen, legislators, and sheriffs. White officeholders were becoming more racially cautious. In much of the Deep South, beatings and deaths at the hands of the Klans had been the direct cost of each of these steps, but by the end of the 1960s, the costs were being shared.

Into jail went the killers of Colonel Lemuel Penn on the highway outside Athens, Georgia, and of Viola Liuzzo in Lowndes County, Alabama; seven of the murderers of Mickey Schwerner, James Chaney, and Andrew Goodman in Neshoba County, Mississippi; and four of the men responsible for the firebombing death of Mississippi black leader Vernon Dahmer. Klansmen were arrested for plotting the murder of Charles Evers, the newly elected black mayor of Fayette, Mississippi. Byron De La Beckwith, whom earlier juries had failed to convict for the sniper murder of Charles's brother Medgar, went to jail for the planned bombing attempt on the Jewish Anti-Defamation League (ADL) leader in New Orleans. So did Tommy Tarrants after a shootout cost the life of the young teacher Kathy Ainsworth. South Carolina Grand Dragon Robert Scoggins and United Klans' Imperial Wizard Shelton served time in federal prisons for refusing to provide Klan records to the HUAC. Robert Miles, the grand dragon of Michigan and future Christian Identity leader, and four of his followers went to jail for bombing school buses in Pontiac, Michigan. Each conviction and imprisonment sapped the energy of Klansmen and the reputation and strength of their organizations. Although federal juries were more likely to convict than were state juries, local and state police were increasingly willing to take action against Klansmen.

· 12 ·

Birmingham's 16th Street Baptist Church & the Black Jesus

*I*t was the disappearance of Schwerner, Chaney, and Goodman in Neshoba County, Mississippi, that was responsible for the redefinition of the FBI's general mission in relation to the Ku Klux Klan. While the FBI had worked on bombing cases elsewhere in the South, J. Edgar Hoover and the bureau had not been much interested in civil rights or the Klan. Hoover had explained to an earlier attorney general that the bureau should not be giving so much attention to "investigating murders, lynching, and assaults, particularly in the Southern states" because it only stirred up agitation.

From 1964 on, the FBI took an active role that was essential in securing the evidence and testimony that sent Klansmen to jail—and there was more. In 1956, the FBI began a program of illegal surveillance and sabotage against the Communist and Socialist Workers Parties, to which it added Martin Luther King Jr., Black Power movements, and the New Left. In the summer of 1964, the FBI further added seventeen Klans and six other hate groups to the "disrupt and neutralize" efforts of its covert Internal Security Counterintelligence Program, known as COUNTERINTELPRO. With Hoover's approval, the program set out to "take advantage of our experience with a variety of sophisticated techniques successfully applied against the Communist Party USA." The "sophisticated techniques" included not only the use of informers and theft of Klan records but also all manner of planted newspaper stories, rumors, anonymous letters, and postcards revealing Klan membership and accusing Klan leaders of everything from drunkenness, adultery, and misuse of funds to being informers for the

FBI itself. Favored newspapermen, such as the *Atlanta Constitution*'s Ralph McGill, were leaked information. By the 1970s, the bureau claimed that one out of every six Klansmen worked for the FBI. This included at least one state leader, and there was talk of attempting to dethrone the United Klan's imperial wizard, Robert Shelton, and replace him with an FBI informant.

Though the program was successful in stirring up trouble within the klaverns, Hoover feared that its illegal operations might become known to the public. His fears were realized in 1971,

Postcard messages sent to the Ku Klux Klansmen by the FBI

when an antiwar group calling itself the Citizens Commission to Investigate the FBI broke into an FBI office in Media, Pennsylvania, and began making public the contents of the FBI surveillance files. The Media burglary did not reveal the existence of COUNTERINTELPRO, but Hoover cautiously closed it down. Four years later, an NBC reporter, Carl Stern, heard about the program and used the Freedom of Information Act to find out more about it. Hoover had died in 1972, and now a U.S. Senate investigation, chaired by Idaho's Senator Frank Church, revealed something of COUNTERINTELPRO's extent. A new freedom-of-information suit by a group of reporters made public some 52,000 pages and began a long battle over access and preservation of FBI records.

Sharing the headlines with the wiretapping and the FBI campaign to discredit Martin Luther King Jr. was the portly figure of the bureau's onetime top Klan informant, Gary Thomas Rowe Jr. Of the bureau's more than 1,000 "domestic intelligence informants," Rowe was the star. Recruited in 1960, he surfaced five years later to finger the Klansman who had gunned down Viola Liuzzo on the road between Selma and Montgomery. Rowe had been one of the men in the killer's car, and his testimony sent two brother Klansmen to federal prison. Wearing a mask that resembled a torn paper bag, Rowe told congressmen that he had been in on almost everything, from beating the "freedom riders" in Birmingham to an FBI-ordered disruption campaign by having sexual relations with the wives of fellow Klansmen. And there was more, including beatings, perhaps a murder, and, the word was to come later from the Birmingham police, possible involvement in the 1963 bombing of the 16th Street Baptist Church.

Between 1960, when he was first recruited by the FBI, and 1965, when he broke cover to testify in the Liuzzo trial, Rowe was paid more than $20,000 by the bureau, first for information and then to relocate with a new identity—hence the mask. Although his cover was destroyed by his testimony, Rowe profited from the exposure. Bantam Books reportedly paid him and his ghostwriter $25,000 for a slim paperback autobiography titled *My Undercover Years with the Ku Klux Klan*. The book was characterized by the kind of writing that fills the pages of magazines for men, replete with exclamatory verbs and virile conversation but lacking any sort of modifying description or understanding. According to his literary testimony, Rowe had bested—and outwitted—his brother Klansmen of Birmingham's fearsome Eastview Klavern 13 in drinking, fighting, and sexual conquests.

Before concern began to mount about the nature of the violence that Rowe himself had perpetrated while on government retainer, Columbia Pictures added $25,000 to his take for the rights to film his life for NBC television. Football broadcaster and former Dallas Cowboys quarterback "Dandy" Don Meredith played Rowe as a rough but well-meaning battler for the law. NBC swallowed hard and presented its somewhat tarnished drama, *The Freedom Riders,* in the fall of 1979. Meanwhile, the Justice Department was being forced to face the question of whether Rowe had been an agent provocateur. Had he actually instigated the incidents of violence, and had the FBI approved and covered up his actions? Rowe claimed that they had and that he was told that J. Edgar Hoover approved.

Three court suits against the U.S. government, all of them on behalf of white victims, came out of Rowe's role as the FBI's most valuable informer. He had told the FBI about the violence planned against the freedom riders, and now two of the riders who had sustained permanent damage from the beatings claimed that the government had failed in its duty to protect them. Federal judges agreed and awarded James Peck $25,000 and Walter Bergman $50,000. Viola Liuzzo's family was less fortunate. The Klan plans were less definite, and the judged ruled that the government had not been negligent. The Liuzzo family would get no damages, and they would have had to pay the government's $80,000 court costs if it had not been for an angry story on ABC television's *20/20* and the intercession of two U.S. senators. The crucial two-sided question was over the responsibility of the government to protect people when it knows that violence is coming as opposed to its interests in protecting its sources. In addition, there was often the additional question of the FBI sharing what it knew, which was to affect prosecution of 1960s murders for the next forty years.

No one loves an informer, including police officers who employ him, but without him the hands of justice would often be tied. Contrary to the heroic image put forth by motion pictures and television, it is seldom the police officer who infiltrates. Rather, it is the member who informs, whether out of patriotism, morality, revenge, a desire to escape prosecution himself, or a need for money. It was informers such as Rowe (plus testimony of frightened or penitent Klansmen) and painstaking investigative work that combined to produce the FBI's success against the Klan.

Of the killings that marked the struggle of the 1960s, the deaths of the four black teenagers in the bombing of Birmingham's 16th Street Baptist Church remained the chief unsolved crime. Within days after the dynamite bomb went off against the wall of the church, federal agents were sure that they knew who set it. However, the problems of surveillance and gathering evidence were soon overtaken by the need to protect the evidence from misuse. Alabama Governor George Wallace had taken as strong a stand as anyone against integration, but the church bombing murders were hardly the kind of publicity he was counting on to launch his campaign for president. Martin Luther King Jr.'s telegraph message, "The blood of our little children is on your hands," was sure to upset voters. After an unsuccessful attempt to somehow pin the bombing on "unknown black perpetrators," the governor's investigators arrested the FBI's prime suspects. The best that the state could do was to charge Klansman "Dynamite Bob" Chambliss with the illegal possession of dynamite. The prime suspects were now warned, and the bombing went into the "unsolved" file. Rowe later claimed that this was where the Alabama state police and the Klan intended it to stay.

Murder has no statute of limitations in Alabama, and a rising young lawyer named William Baxley kept this in mind. He first heard about the bombing while at his Kappa Sigma fraternity house on the University of Alabama campus in nearby Tuscaloosa. It made him sick to his stomach, and he said that he did not eat that day. Son of a prominent judge from Dothan and a mother deeply involved with her church, Baxley had a sense of justice that did not condone racism or unpunished murder. With his law school classmates helping him organize his statewide campaign, he rose from being a local state's attorney to attorney general of Alabama by the time he was thirty. When he came up for reelection in 1974, no one thought it worthwhile to run against him.

After his first election, Baxley reportedly wrote four names on his state telephone card. They were Cynthia Wesley, Denise Mc-Nair, Carol Robertson, and Addie Mae Collins. Denise McNair was eleven and the others were fourteen years old when they died in the bomb blast. That had been eight years before, but Baxley had not forgotten them, and now he saw their names whenever he used his state telephone card. It took four more years and threats of newspaper publicity before the FBI would begin making their files available. It was not without justification that the FBI had been hesitant in 1963 about revealing its evidence and informants to the Alabama police. Now Baxley's sincerity impressed them.

Of at least equal importance was the death of J. Edgar Hoover in 1972. Hoover had rescued the FBI from the bad reputation of its 1920s corruption but had plunged it into even deeper scandal in the 1950s and 1960s. Shortly after the bombing of the 16th Street Baptist Church and some fourteen years before Alabama's Attorney General Baxley would bring one of the bombers to trial, the FBI had cracked the case and had strong evidence against Robert Chambliss and at least three other men who had helped set the dynamite. Hoover had twice refused the Birmingham office permission to seek prosecution and told it not to let the Justice Department suspect how much the FBI knew.

After finally seeing what he thought were all the FBI files, Baxley believed that there had been enough evidence to go to trial within weeks of the bombing, though Hoover may well have been correct in his assumption that in 1963 the all-white juries of Birmingham were not likely to convict, even for such a heinous crime as this. By 1977, the man believed to have made the bomb was dead. Baxley's staff pressed the investigation. In September 1977, an Alabama grand jury indicted Chambliss on four accounts of first-degree murder.

Baxley hoped that Gary Rowe would strengthen the case against Chambliss and others involved in the bombing, but Rowe's lie detector tests produced disturbing results. When questioned about the bombing, Rowe's polygraph reading indicated "strong and consistent unresolved deceptive responses." Rowe, it seemed, was telling less than all he knew. Baxley's investigators began to suspect that Rowe might have been in the car that carried the bombers to the church. At the very least, the trial would have to go on without Rowe as a witness for the prosecution.

The trial was held before a jury made up of three black and nine white jurors. Most of the latter were middle-aged, working-class housewives. The evidence was circumstantial but powerful. Chambliss's niece by marriage, now a Methodist minister in Birmingham, testified that Chambliss, whom she called "a racial fanatic," was angry over integration in the Birmingham schools. He had "enough stuff out away to flatten half of Birmingham," he told her. "You just wait until after Sunday morning, and they will beg us to let them segregate." Another witness had wandered into a room in the Chambliss house and seen his store of dynamite, piled like "oversized firecrackers." A Birmingham policeman remembered Chambliss describing how to make a "drip bomb," in which a fishing float would complete the circuit and set off the explosives when enough water had dripped out of a leaking bucket. An FBI expert testified that light objects frequently survived and that a fishing float had been found after the explosion. Chambliss was identified as having been seated in a parked car across the street early in the morning of the explosion. Chambliss's niece told of her uncle watching a television program about the bombing and protesting, "It wasn't meant to hurt anybody; it didn't go off when it was supposed to."

Chambliss did not take the stand. His attorney was Arthur Hanes Jr., whose father had been mayor of Birmingham in 1963 and later defended the accused murderers of Viola Liuzzo. Hanes had worked with his father on the Liuzzo case and had been an attorney for the killer of Martin Luther King Jr., James Earl Ray. Hanes argued that the charges against Chambliss were not proven. Everyone "talked rough" in those days, he explained. Baxley's summation for the prosecution lasted ninety minutes and brought many of the jurors to tears. "You've got a chance to do something," he told them. "Let the world know that this is not the way the people of Alabama felt then or feel now."

The decision was not easy for the jury, the foreman related, and it had taken nearly all the evidence to convince them. After six hours, they brought in a verdict of guilty of murder in the first degree. In the Alabama justice system, Chambliss's life sentence meant a minimum of ten years in prison before he would be eligible for parole. "This is a terrible thing to do to a seventy-three-year-old man," he complained.

Attorney General Baxley repeatedly stated that Chambliss had not acted alone and promised additional arrests for the more than fifty bombings that had shaken Birmingham during the 1960s. The grand jury that had named Chambliss also indicted National States Rights Party lawyer J. B. Stoner for another of the bombings. No one had as many connections in the Klan world as Stoner, who once commented that Hitler had been "too moderate." For more than three decades, Stoner carried his message of hatred for Jews and black people to the klaverns of the hooded knights and defended their members when they got in trouble.

Aware of the propaganda opportunities that arise during elections, Stoner repeatedly ran for office, often gaining a respectable number of votes. During one gubernatorial race in Georgia, Jerry Ray, the brother of Martin Luther King Jr.'s assassin, had managed Stoner's campaign. Facing extradition to Alabama, where placing a bomb against an inhabited dwelling constituted a capital crime, Stoner had an even greater incentive to be elected. As governor of Georgia, he could claim to be fully within his rights in refusing to extradite himself to stand trial in Alabama. When the Federal Communications Commission ruled that it was also within his rights to say what he wanted in his campaign, he infuriated many Atlantans with television spots denouncing integration as "a nigger plot" to take over white women. "You cannot have law and order and niggers too," his political ads proclaimed. However, the man elected governor was not Stoner. Instead, Stoner had to face the new breed of law and order in Birmingham, which proceeded to convict him. In 1980, Stoner was sentenced to ten years in prison for the 1958 bombing of Birmingham's Bethel Baptist Church. He served six years before his release, part of them as Chambliss's cell mate. In 1985, Chambliss died in prison.

Denise McNair's father was elected to the Alabama legislature. A black lawyer whose house had been bombed became a member of the Birmingham City Council. In the fall of 1979, the voters elected a black man mayor of Birmingham. At the 16th Street Baptist Church, where the stained-glass window of the sanctuary depicts a black Christ hanging on his cross, a memorial plaque contains the pictures of Denise McNair, Cynthia Wesley, Carol Robertson, and Addie Mae Collins smiling. The inscription reads, "May men learn to replace bitterness and violence with love and understanding."

· 13 ·

Confrontation, Poor-Boy Politics, & Revival in the Late 1970s

𝕋he 1970s did not seem very promising for the Ku Klux Klan. Although Klansmen might have the weapons and the will for "a little action," the chances of being caught were becoming much too high, and the behavior of judges and juries was downright discouraging. Still, the various competing, though shrunken, hooded empires, peopled by Klansmen, Klanswomen, and FBI informants, continued to rally and parade in Walker, Louisiana; Pensacola, Florida; Macon and Stone Mountain, Georgia; Aurora, Illinois; and Chenango County, New York; and to burn occasional crosses in New Jersey and school buses in Pontiac, Michigan. Attempts were made to project a better image. Klansmen would "light up" a cross rather than "burn" one because that sounded more respectful. Attorney James Venable's National Knights and David Duke's Knights dropped their bans against Roman Catholics. Duke, a young Louisiana State University history graduate, carried his message to the college campuses and told working-class listeners in South Boston that the Klan would help them "protect, preserve, and advance the white race." A real celebrity, the lovely woman jockey Mary Bacon made the television evening news and lost most of her contracts for endorsements by revealing her Klan membership. "We are not just a bunch of illiterate southern nigger killers," she reassured her fellow Klanspeople. "We are good white Christian people, hard-working people working for a white America." She added, "When one of your wives or one of your sisters gets raped by a nigger, maybe you'll get smart and join the Klan."

The newly elected grand dragon of a splinter Texas Klan

attributed his success to a Dale Carnegie course, and an Indiana grand dragon complained about Klansmen showing up at rallies out of uniform: "If you join the Shrine you buy a fez, or the 40 & 8, you get a chapeau. . . . If you can't afford a robe," he sputtered, "you can't afford to belong to the Klan." The Klans survived, but their ranks seemed destined to remain depleted. There was almost a melancholy note to the Florida grand dragon's explanation that the Klan existed because "the white people has rights just like anybody else."

And then, at the end of the 1970s, something happened. There was a dramatic increase in the number of cross burnings, rallies, marches, confrontations, and shootings. Klan ranks grew. In 1978, the Jewish watchdog Anti-Defamation League (ADL), which for a generation has known at least as much about the Klans as the Klans themselves, called it "a minor renaissance." By the next year, the ADL reported not only an increase in visibility but also impressive proportionate gains in membership. Since mid-decade, Klan membership had increased from some 6,500 to 10,000. Perhaps more significant, Klan approval and support appeared to have grown substantially. In the media, television commentators and editorial writers announced "the Klan revival" and talked of "the New Klan" and "the amazing rebirth." The wire services and the press reported, "Klan hasn't folded up its sheets," "Klan's growing militancy reminiscent of sixties," and "Klan rises again in the South."

What had really happened? Ten thousand Klansmen and Klanswomen were not a large number out of the 225 million Americans or even of some seventy million southerners. They did not compare in power with the several hundred thousand Reconstruction-era Klansmen, the millions of the second Klan during the 1920s, or even the thousands that the "third-era" Klans mustered during the civil rights battles of the 1960s. Since Doc Samuel Green's death in 1949, no one had been able to unite the Klans and rule an undivided empire as Hiram Wesley Evans, William J. Simmons, and Confederate Cavalry General Nathan Bedford Forrest had done in times past. Revival did not mean unity, and Klan ranks remained thin.

The "fourth-era" revival of the Klans was a matter of place, confrontation, and economic anxiety. Its home was in the towns and smaller southern industrial cities. The confrontations that took place in northern Mississippi and Alabama—Tupelo, Holly Springs, Byhalia, Lexington, Corinth, Okolona, Elkmont, Moulton, Court-land, Huntsville, Cullman, Tarrant City, Fairfield, and Decatur— were not of the old pre-1960s variety. Although the fading Klan entrepreneur of Stone Mountain, James Venable, might complain about "niggers calling white girls by their first names," the day of punishing the "uppity" black was gone.

In bygone times, the Klan patrolled the borders of race rela-tions in the South. Now the erosion of those borders had produced a limited but potentially deadly Klan revival as an expressive form of poor-boy politics. Its essence was the inability of the rural-minded southern working-class white to either prevent or accept racial change. It was this powerlessness that caused the revived Klans to play the game of violence as an expressive alternative to actual power for controlling larger events.

In the renewed world of Klandom at the end of the 1970s, Bill Wilkinson's "Invisible Empire" was the most militant. What hap-pened was actually a version of the standard scenario. Police vio-lence and questions about the quality of justice meted out to black people would produce a protest that would grow to include issues of jobs and poverty. An organization would then be formed, and its members would take to the streets to march on city hall and perhaps boycott downtown merchants. Wilkinson would come to town to encourage white resistance and Klan recruitment. Black and Klan demonstrators would jostle each other in the streets. Crosses would be burned. Nighttime rallies would draw applaud-ing spectators and new members for the Klan. Since everyone was armed, there would be incidents in the streets and on country roads, and shots would be fired into the homes of black and some-times white leaders.

As downtown business suffered, mayors would say, "Why us? We've always gotten along so well!" Klansmen from neighboring counties, civil rights marchers from Atlanta, and agents from the Justice Department in Washington would arrive. Efforts to ban marches would be declared in violation of the First Amendment to the Constitution. At high cost to municipal budgets, riot police with bulletproof vests and shotguns, aided by state troopers and an occasional patrol helicopter, would keep blacks and Klansmen apart and marches separate. With the help of civil rights lawyers, now often black and federally funded, the black protesters would usually win the courtroom battles. The Justice Department's Community Relations Service would help city commissions make rules for marches and public meetings and ban the carrying of weapons by marchers or spectators. With mediation, compromises, some arrests and convictions, and numerous suspended sentences, confrontations would simmer down to hostile standoffs and ultimately an uneasy peace.

Black men killed by police officers, testimony of rape and beatings in county jails, a "suicide" found hanging in his cell with hands and feet bound, and the refusal of local government and juries to act moved black protest into the streets of northern Mississippi. Alfred "Skip" Robinson had begun to organize his United League of Mississippi in the mid-1960s, and it remained a 1960s-type civil rights organization. Its members wore T-shirts that read "Justice for All," not "Black Power." Robinson, a brick mason and contractor in Holly Springs, was a stubborn man who had dedicated his life to organizing his people and, said his white detractors, seeking office and political power. The United League was anchored in the black churches. Robinson spoke to them in the language they understood, and they cheered him as he told them "my knees won't bend."

To their demands that the police officers accused of beating black prisoners be fired, the United League added that city governments and white merchants must hire more black people. Marches for justice and boycotts for black jobs damaged business in Okolona and Tupelo, raised community tempers, and brought in the Klan and the national media. Local and state politicians denounced the Klan as "a bunch of hoods covered up with a sheet" and not representative of the people of Mississippi, but the crowds at Imperial Wizard Wilkinson's rallies grew, and they cheered as he promised to "restore this government to the white people."

Klansmen attacked black marchers in Tupelo and Okolona and shot at cars on the highways outside town at night. In many Mississippi towns, there were token black councilmen and school board members, and the politicians and merchants were inclined to seek compromise with the black demands. However, neither action nor inaction was likely to satisfy the United League or the Klansmen. As a city councilman commented, Tupelo was a stage on which a potentially violent drama was being acted out.

It was Alabama that gave Wilkinson's Invisible Empire its biggest chance. A young retarded black man named Tommy Lee Hines was accused of robbing and raping three white women. Many members of the black community felt that Hines, whose I.Q. was only thirty-nine, was incapable of such actions as driving the car involved in the abduction. The Reverend R. B. Cottonreader organized protest marches, and a "Justice City" tent community camp-in on the Decatur City Hall lawn brought Klan leader Wilkinson to town. His aggressive rhetoric drew crowds of 5,000 and then 10,000 people to the biggest rallies that anyone could remember since the great days of the 1920s. Wilkinson seemed to have discovered the way to build Klan power, and he meant to make the most of it. In a trial that had been moved to nearby Cullman, an all-white jury found Hines guilty, and he was sentenced to thirty years in jail. A reversal on appeal for Hines, plus other trials coming up, meant a prolonged season of protest and counterprotest. However, the confrontation was moving beyond Hines.

Imperial Wizard Wilkinson's style was one of tough talk and a display of weaponry. Although he might look benign with his large "mod" Gloria Steinem glasses and slightly rotund figure dressed in a three-piece blue suit and his belted and booted, uniformed bodyguards, with their pistols, rifles, shotguns, and Thompson submachine guns, looked anything but peaceful. As one Alabaman described him, Wilkinson was a "gun-toting, cigar-chewing, cow-pasture Klansman, a man unafraid of action, proud to be a redneck."

Klansmen and black demonstrators clashed in the parking lot outside a supermarket where a black man had been arrested for shoplifting. Having already banned tent cities from the lawn, the Decatur City Council forbade the carrying of weapons at a demonstration. The Klan responded with a nighttime motorcade of pickup trucks past the mayor's house, with the drivers waving their rifles. "If the mayor wants our guns, he'll have to come and get them," a Klan leader proclaimed.

Black demonstrators, led by Southern Christian Leadership Conference President Joseph Lowery, came up from Atlanta to support Reverend Cottonreader. The black marchers found their route blocked by a line of Klansmen with lead pipes, ax handles, and baseball bats who shouted, "Niggers, that's as far as you go!" In the melee that followed, the Decatur police tried to keep the groups apart. There was a pistol shot in the direction of the Klansmen, followed by an erratic exchange of fire in which the police also joined.

Although no one could have foreseen it, the Decatur confrontation was to be catastrophic for the Klan world. Curtis Robinson was not one of the marchers, but inadvertently he had been caught up in its traffic jam. Now he was on trial for firing a pistol at a Klansman who had menaced his family. Lawyer Morris Dees of the Southern Poverty Law Center (SPLC) came up from Montgomery to defend Robinson and became concerned over the revived activity of the Klan. As a result, Dees set up a "Klanwatch" in the SPLC to track and litigate against the Klan. From this came a powerful new weapon. Beginning with the Decatur street confrontation, the SPLC's Klanwatch began suing various Klans in federal court for civil rights violations, seeking damage awards so great that they could put the Klan out of business.

The new role of the SPLC was not immediately felt as club-carrying Klansmen in the municipal building hallways stamped their feet and shouted, "white power!" The Klan summer of 1979 was launched in northern Alabama. Weekends meant cross burnings and rallies, and Klansmen stopped cars on the roads at night to collect donations "to fight the niggers." State and FBI investigations led to conviction of Klansmen for shooting into homes of black leaders and interracial couples as the violence spread to the central part of the state. Nighttime gunshots were becoming a part of life, but heavily armed police managed to keep peace as Klansmen and black protesters paraded separately through Decatur.

The state of Alabama passed a law forbidding firearms within 1,000 feet of a public demonstration. When in August 1979 Wilkinson's Invisible Empire decided to repeat Martin Luther King

Jr.'s famous 1965 march from Selma to Montgomery, the police were waiting for them at the Montgomery city line. If the Klan ranks, which had swelled to more than 170, were somewhat less impressive than the 10,000 who had marched into Montgomery with King, they made up for it in armament. The pile of weapons confiscated by the police at the entrance to the Klan's campsite included pistols, rifles, chains, knives, bayonets, brass knuckles, and a submachine gun. When the marchers crossed the city line the next day, they were arrested for parading without a permit.

How had the Klansmen felt when their march took them past the spot where Viola Liuzzo died fourteen years before? There was no remorse apparent. "She was doing an unsanctimonious thing, helping those niggers," Imperial Wizard Wilkinson explained. What had been the purpose of the Klan march? "To protect the civil rights of white people," he said. Martin Luther King Jr.'s marchers had been permitted to rally on the capitol steps in Montgomery, but Wilkinson's demonstrators were arrested for parading without a permit. The difference in treatment symbolized what the Klan was protesting. The Klan's working-class constituency believed that a reversal had taken place in America. The black man had been elevated, and the white man had taken his place in the ditch. Wilkinson summed up the theme sounded on every Klan platform when he attacked government programs, saying, "I for one am sick of Negroes and other minorities being given jobs I deserve."

While the Klan revival was limited, it represented a lingering racism in American society. It sprang from an unwillingness to accept the changing role of black people and from the conditions and conflicts that were the result. Confrontation over justice and jobs in northern Mississippi and Alabama produced the kind of racist response that gave impetus to the upswing in the cycle of Klan membership. Behind the clashes in Tupelo and Decatur was the old populist resentment and suspicion that times were not going to be good and that jobs and promotions were going to someone else. That that someone was black was too much to accept. Integration, welfare, affirmative action, hard times, and Reverend Cottonreader's tent city blacks camped out on the city hall lawn and throwing beer cans into the shrubbery because a black man was convicted for raping a white woman were more than a white man should be asked to bear. There was enough feeling in enough people so that when David Duke, Bill Wilkinson, or Bobby Shelton could call out, "What do we want?" they responded, "White Power!" "What?" "White Power . . . *White Power!*"

While there was a broader audience for the Klan's issues, the expansion of various Klan organizations was much more limited. In addition to the pressure from Dees and the SPLC, Klan leaders often ran into other difficulties. In 1981, someone leaked to the Nashville *Tennessean* that Wilkinson had long been an FBI informant, and his Klan evaporated.

· 14 ·

Death in Greensboro

Greensboro was a middle-sized industrial city in the North Carolina piedmont. Despite its five colleges, the first response of North Carolinians when asked to describe the city was "blue collar." In addition to P. Lorillard tobacco and Vics chemicals, there are the textile mills—Burlington, J. P. Stevens, and Cone Mills—which each year produced enough denim to more than cover the entire state of North Carolina. The approaches to Greensboro were thick with the typical fast-food restaurants, gas stations, used-car dealerships, and suburban shopping centers. The aging downtown buildings of the immediate post–World War II boom, none higher than eight stories, did not give a distinctive skyline or feeling.

Greensboro's main claim to fame was that General Nathanael Greene turned back the British there at the battle of Guilford Courthouse and started General Cornwallis on his retreat to the Yorktown surrender that ensured American independence. Such history was favored by most city boosters, for the distant past tended not to offend, but the name of Greensboro joined those of Montgomery, Oxford, Albany, Birmingham, Selma, Memphis, and the other southern cities where the racial history of America has been written.

North Carolinians liked to say that "moderation" has been the keynote of relations between blacks and whites in their state. By the 1950s, Greensboro had already elected a black city councilman, and there was a black member on the school board. When Governor Luther Hodges spoke to the black student body of North Carolina Agricultural and Technical State University (hereafter A&T), he urged them to keep things cool by following a policy of voluntary

115

segregation, and state legislators saw token integration as the way to maintain separation of the races.

In 1956, Martin Luther King Jr. and the black bus boycotters had walked to victory in Montgomery, Alabama, but civil rights did not become a mass movement until February 1, 1960, when four nervous but determined black freshmen sat down at Greensboro's Woolworth lunch counter. David Richmond, Franklin McCain, Joseph McNeil, and Ezell Blair Jr. had hatched the idea during a dormitory bull session the night before. It had been stimulated, however, by nights of such talk at group meetings of the National Association for the Advancement of Colored People, a growing awareness of black history, the Montgomery example, Martin Luther King Jr.'s speech at A&T, and the fact that Joseph McNeil had been refused service at the Greensboro Trailways bus terminal lunch counter.

The sit-ins spread across the South. They flowed into the "freedom rides"; into the streets of Albany, Birmingham, St. Augustine, and Selma; on to the back roads of Mississippi; and into the national civil rights laws. They set in motion the movement of black people into the politics and mainstream of southern life. With it all came a furious response and then the decline of the Ku Klux Klan. Once black people became a factor in southern politics, white politicians toned down their rhetoric, white sheriffs began to be somewhat more restrained, and some black legislators, policemen, and sheriffs began to appear among the white ones. Andrew Young, a promising young black minister turned congressman from Atlanta, summed it up:

> When not many black people could vote, the politicians used to talk about "the niggers." When we got 10 to 15 percent voting, they called us "nigras." When we got up to 25 percent, they learned how to say "Nee-gro." Now that we have 60 to 70 percent registered and voting, they say how happy they are to see "so many black brothers and sisters here tonight."

On February 1, 1980, twenty years after the Woolworth sit-in, there was a civil ceremony in Greensboro. With the mayor looking on, David Richmond, Franklin McCain, Joseph McNeil, and Jibreel Khazan (formerly Ezell Blair Jr.) were welcomed at the lunch counter by Woolworth's black manager, and historical markers were unveiled outside.

Even so, it had not been easy in Greensboro. "Moderation" meant maintaining things as they were. Although kept out of the national headlines, under pressure from the students at A&T, Bennett College for Women, and occasionally the white colleges, Greensboro experienced a decade of sit-ins, demonstrations, mass arrests, and confrontations with the Klan. On the day that the Woolworth sit-in was honored, a memorial to a student who had been shot during a National Guard sweep of the campus in 1969 was unveiled at A&T. In the mid-1960s, the student leader at A&T was Jesse Jackson. During the even more difficult times later in the decade, the student leader was an Air Force veteran named Nelson Johnson. It was not until 1971 that the Greensboro public schools were integrated, among the last in the South. Jackson had gone off to Chicago, and Johnson remained, working with the poor in Greensboro.

Across the nation on February 1, 1980, the media retold the story of the original Woolworth lunch counter sit-in that had touched off the Civil Rights movement of the 1960s. People spoke with pride about the racial progress that had resulted. The next day, February 2, in a plot twist that might have intrigued Greensboro's famous native son, the writer O. Henry, more than 5,000 angry people, black and white, took to the streets in a new racial protest. They had come from Chicago and Detroit, from the eastern seaboard cities, and from the South to protest the killing of four white men and a black woman by a band of Klansmen and Nazis in the streets of Greensboro.

Shortly before noon on Saturday, November 3, 1979, a nine-car caravan worked its way into the narrow streets of Greensboro's black district, where an anti-Klan rally was forming in front of the Morningside Homes at Everitt and Carver Streets. There were shouted insults. Demonstrators in the street pounded on the cars with sticks and clubs. Someone in the lead car fired a pistol into the air. Then, as television camera crews filmed away, half a dozen men climbed out of a sedan and a yellow van in the rear of the procession, opened the trunk of the sedan, and took out rifles and shotguns.

With cigarettes dangling from their lips, they leaned over the hood of the car and opened fire on a shrieking, scattering crowd of men, women, and children at a distance of no more than twenty-five feet. Within seconds, the wounded and dying lay bleeding in the street. Of the dead and dying, one was a Duke University computer operator, and three were doctors, graduates of Duke and the University of Chicago and Virginia medical schools. The black woman had been student body president at Bennett College.

At the end of the 1970s, there were no large-scale left- or right-wing groups in America, but there were many fragments at both ends of the political spectrum. Two of them had met violently in the streets of Greensboro. For several years, a devoted Maoist group who called themselves the Workers Viewpoint Organization (WVO) had been attempting to organize the Greensboro textile mills. Working part time in clinics and hospital emergency rooms or hiding their education and professions in order to get jobs at Cone Mills or J. P. Stevens, they sought to lead "the struggles of oppressed people" and the coming anticapitalist revolution. One of the doctors killed in the shooting had been president of his textile union; another was a shop steward and was running for union president. The leader of the group, who survived the fusillade of Klan and Nazi bullets, was the integrationist battler of the 1960s, Nelson Johnson.

Like radical idealists of times past, the WVO members had given up promising careers to work and live among the poor. They saw the working classes as the essential revolutionary element and had gone to the mills to reach and radicalize them. They had been "turned off" by the system. In their study groups, reading and discussions had convinced them that the revolutionary moment was at hand. For them, the capitalist system was violent, and therefore the struggle against it could not be nonviolent. In Durham and Greensboro, they worked with the black poor, with the university and hospital service workers, and in the mills. It would be difficult, but, they believed, the working classes would rise.

By the summer of 1979, the WVO was having trouble in the mills. Despite the heat, the deafening noise, and the fiber-filled air that caused brown lung disease, the management position was strong. No one had yet organized the southern mills, even for trade union goals. The WVO were well liked, but they were caught between management and the national union. The Amalgamated Cotton Textile Workers Union (ACTWU) did not wish to share the labor movement, slim though it was, with the revolution. The National Labor Relations Board upheld the dismissal of WVO member Dr. James Waller for omitting his medical degree from his job application at Cone Mills, and the national ACTWU had taken over direction of Cone Mills locals on the grounds that the elected officers did not properly represent all the workers.

Squeezed between capital and labor, the WVO seemed very much in need of new tactics. They changed their name to the Communist Workers Party (CWP) and challenged the Klan. The newly renamed CWP clashed with the Klan at nearby China Grove, burned a Klan banner, and disrupted a Klan showing of the film *The Birth of a Nation*. A "Death to the Klan" march was scheduled for November 3 and was well advertised. Open letters to the leaders of the White Knights of Liberty and to the Federated Knights of the Ku Klux Klan announced that Klan cowardice would be further exposed by the march. "Death to the Klan!" The CWP would "physically smash the racist KKK wherever it reared its ugly head."

There were at least five competing Klans in North Carolina, and those Klansmen who did not find the various "Invisible Empires" active enough often wound up in one of the even smaller National Socialist or Nazi parties. The Klansmen and Nazis who drove into Greensboro in the caravan that Saturday morning were mainly mill workers or laborers, in their thirties, from around Winston–Salem and small towns in Lincoln County on the South Carolina line. Concerned about "saving America" from race-mixing Communism and such, many of them were new to Klandom. As the *New York Times'* Wayne King described it, "These guys are not what you'd call real successful."

When Joe Grady, leader of the White Knights, chose not to accept the CWP's invitation to "face the wrath of the people," rival Klan leader Virgil Griffin decided that this was his chance. His Invisible Empire had been meeting with the National Socialists to work out a United Racist Front, and he brought some of his Nazi allies along with him. They intended to show the Communists that they were not going to let anyone call them cowards.

A third party to it all, though not consulted, was the black housing project neighborhood where the rally was to begin. A fourth party was the police. The anti-Klan marchers had promised not to carry weapons, had filed the route of the parade, and had been given a permit. The CWP publicized its rally and march. When a Klansman asked for the route plan, the city attorney ruled that it was a public document, and he was given a copy. Twenty-six men under the direction of a black officer were assigned to keep things orderly, and the police had an informant among the Klansmen and Nazis who came in that morning on the interstate highway. As the starting time approached, the police found rallies going on in two different places. No one would give information to the sergeant, who checked out the Morningside Homes site, and the crowd added a "fascist pig" chant to their denunciations of the Klan. The police were split between the two locations, and the sergeant decided to avoid provocation and keep his men at a distance from the Morningside housing project. With the warning to be on post by half an hour before the start of the march, some of the men were given permission to go for food.

There were thirty to thirty-five Klansmen and Nazis. Having come to town early, they had been standing around and were eager to get going. Although the police had been informed that their intent was to heckle, some of them had weapons. According to the police report afterward, there had been no legal grounds for stopping and detaining them. Some eight cars started out, and a ninth joined them. It was forty minutes before parade time, and a number of the police officers had not yet come back from eating. The Klansmen claimed that they had intended to leave their rifles and shotguns behind in the trunk of Ray Caudle's Ford sedan. This would have left them armed only with the six dozen eggs they had bought on the way. One of the Klansmen took the Ford and went off for food, but the rest were impatient, so someone got on the citizens-band radio and called him back. The Klan caravan started out, and the Ford sedan with the weapons in its trunk joined at the end of the line.

By the time the police caught up with the caravan, four people were dead, one was dying, and the wounded were scattered on the street outside Morningside Homes. It took less than two minutes for the police to arrive, and the ambulances followed soon after. The yellow van was stopped, and twelve Klansmen and Nazis were arrested. Murder charges were eventually placed against fourteen of the assailants. Presumably on the informant's report that the shooting had not been planned in advance, conspiracy charges were not placed, and the people in the other Klan cars were not arrested. Four days later, the editor of the *Greensboro Daily News* summed it up: "As the fifth victim, a medical doctor turned textile worker died in a Greensboro hospital, his alleged murderers sang 'Onward, Christian Soldiers' and 'My Country 'tis of Thee' in a Greensboro jail." It was both "puzzling," he said, and "tragic."

There was a sense of disbelief and horror in white Greensboro and anger in black communities across the country. For black people in the South, the Klan was a never-ending racial oppression. The grieving CWP survivors blamed the deaths on the police as a "pig-Klan assassination conspiracy." President Jimmy Carter ordered the FBI to investigate. The Southern Christian Leadership Conference (SCLC), locked in conflict with Klansmen in northern Mississippi, Alabama, and Georgia, had already met in Norfolk with representatives of more than thirty organizations to work out a national anti-Klan campaign. Now the SCLC called a major planning session for Atlanta in December.

"The Klan is for real," SCLC President Joseph Lowrey stated, adding that it did not exist in a vacuum. Neither did the anti-Klan protest. The clash in the streets represented larger problems and conflict. The CWP's blood had been shed in a black neighborhood by white racists. The police had knowingly permitted the armed convoy of Klansmen and Nazis to drive into the Morningside Homes area and were not there when the shooting took place. Now "the press and the establishment" were talking about "provocation" and were trying to pass it all off as a shootout between radical fringe groups, and CWP leaders as well as Nazis and Klansmen were under arrest. The problem for black churches and organizations was how to share the protest over Greensboro and opposition to the Klan without becoming too closely associated with the CWP's dangerous martyrs and survivors. One could not fail to be moved by Dale Sampson's quiet, dry-eyed description of her husband's death, but few civil rights leaders wanted to join the call for a Communist revolution in the streets of Greensboro.

An interfaith memorial service filled Greensboro's Bethel Church with an interracial crowd of politicians and concerned citizens, but it was carefully timed to keep it separate from the funeral march for the slain activists. The larger national memorial that took place three months later on February 2 was marked by the same ambivalence. The December planning meeting in Atlanta had focused on the march as a major undertaking for its new Anti-Klan Network. Endorsement, support, and marchers were energetically recruited around the country, but until the last moment, there was a struggle to pledge the CWP not to carry weapons during the procession.

During the march, the CWP contingent pushed forward toward the head of the line, lofting their "AVENGE THE CWP 5" and "DEATH TO THE KLAN" signs as they chanted antipolice slogans at the heavily armed parade escorts. Contingents of protestors, bused in from New York, Ohio, Pennsylvania, Virginia, Tennessee, West Virginia, and Georgia, swelled the number of marchers to close to 7,000, but the absence of many national black and civil rights organizations indicated that the anti-Klan world was perhaps as divided as that of the Invisible Empire.

There had been five people killed and one crippled, all leaders of the CWP, and eight others wounded. None of the dead and wounded had been Klansmen or Nazis. Over the next six years, there were five trials: a state murder trial (*North Carolina v. Fowler*), two conspiracy trials of Nazis who talked of blowing up Greensboro in the event of conviction, a federal civil rights violation trial (*U.S. v. Griffin*), and a civil damages suit, listing Klansmen; Nazis; local, state, and federal agencies; the city of Greensboro, the Chamber of Commerce; and the textile mills as conspiratorial defendants (*Waller v. Butkovich*).

Only the Nazi bomb plotters went to jail. The state's first-degree murder prosecution was well presented, bolstered by the footage that television cameramen had taken of the whole melee, but the state labored under several disadvantages. The defendants had a friend on the jury who worked for their acquittal, and the CWP survivors refused to cooperate with the prosecutors and stood up in court and denounced the conduct of the trial as part of a conspiracy against them. The defense lawyers, as Elizabeth Wheaton sums it up in her book on the Greensboro killings, *Codename Greenkill* (1987), presented their clients as having gone to Morningside Homes "to protest Communism, to stand up for the flag and America." They were just "good ol' boys," the lawyers argued, "who had been provoked beyond endurance and then attacked by gun-wielding Communists." The jury started out with a majority for conviction but on the eighth day came in with a verdict of not guilty.

The subsequent federal case, based on the new 1968 Civil Rights Protection Act (Title 18, Section 245), stumbled over the need to prove a racial motivation for a killing in which four of the five victims were white. Both cases were confused and complicated by the roles of two government undercover agents among the Klansmen and Nazis and by controversy over the analysis of gun sounds taken from the television tapes. It was clear who had fired the killer rifle and shotgun shells, but had the first shots come from the anti-Klan demonstrators? Both sides had their expert witnesses to argue the point. This time the survivors did testify, but it was not helpful. Again the jury brought in verdicts of acquittal.

No Klansman was ever convicted for the killings. In 1985, in the CWP survivors' broad civil suit for damages, the jury concluded that five Klansmen and Nazis, an informant, and two city police officers were liable in the death of one of the five anti-Klan demonstrators and injury to two others. The police fault had been a failure to control their agent within the Klan and to take sufficiently timely action to prevent the shootout. In a confusing distribution of responsibility and payment, the award amounted to close to $400,000. For its part, the city of Greensboro paid a settlement of $351,500.

· 15 ·

David Duke Steps Forward

Bill Wilkinson had served his apprenticeship as principal lieutenant and editor of David Duke's *Crusader* before breaking away in 1975 to build his own Klan. As the result, Duke found his Knights of the Ku Klux Klan facing competition from Wilkinson's new "Invisible Empire" as well as from the senior Klan leader Robert Shelton's somewhat more numerous but fading United Klans. Duke claimed not to be interested in what he called the "illiterate, gun-toting, redneck" kind of Wilkinson's cow-pasture Klandom. Although Duke's Klansmen faced the same kind of troubled economic future, he sought a broader, higher-quality audience. "We're not just a bunch of fools running around in bed sheets," he explained. "We believe that white people in America face discrimination in employment, promotions, scholarships, college entrance, and union admission."

Being a Klan leader and organizing the revival was a demanding, all-consuming business. It involved continuous travel, speaking to large as well as small groups, and the danger of physical violence. Duke dropped the Klan's traditional bars against Roman Catholics and turned away from the usual ladies' auxiliary path, integrating Klanswomen into his ranks instead. Both he and Wilkinson sought to recruit high school students for their Klan youth corps, and Duke distributed leaflets calling on white students to fight for white power against the "black, Chicano, and Yang criminals who break into your lockers and steal your clothes and wallets." Reaching across the country, he and his lieutenants worked the high schools in Buffalo, Chicago, Los Angeles, and San Diego. The young soldiers in the armed services were another quarry.

Although he won no more than a handful of recruits, the publicity payoff was enormous when black and white Marines fought in Camp Pendleton, when there were racial clashes on Charleston- and Norfolk-based supply ships and aircraft carriers, and when crosses were burned at sea.

In the media of the 1970s, Duke became a real pop culture celebrity. He was paid for speaking on college campuses and was sought after for radio and television interviews and talk shows. Through these, he began to win at least a hearing from middle-class America. By contrast, Wilkinson was working the Klan's traditional recruiting ground, the "good old boy" world of bourbon and Coke and pickup trucks with the rifle on the rack. He and Duke parted with the usual bad feelings and dispute over money that traditionally marked the emergence of new entrepreneurs in the competitive Klan world. Wilkinson was practically an illiterate, Duke commented disparagingly, "a man who has never read anything."

Duke was a reader, a new kind of Klansman, and the smooth-est-talking salesman since D. C. Stephenson, Indiana's ambitious grand dragon of the 1920s. But there was a difference: Duke had convictions. Escaping from an increasingly dysfunctional home as a teenager, he hung out in the office of the New Orleans Citizens' Council, reading about segregation and race. In high school, he joined the Klan, and in college, under the influence of the mentor whom he had met at the Citizens' Council, he was reading Gerald L. K. Smith and other anti-Semitic writers. As a boy, Duke developed a fascination with Adolf Hitler (whose birthday he continued to celebrate), World War II, and the Jews. This helped lead him into the tangled world of the American Nazi movement and remained with him on the Louisiana State University campus, in the Klan, and afterward.

Duke was both a racialist and a racist. The unchanging core of his belief was race and the superiority of the Americans of northern European descent. For all others, he felt a contempt that he could never completely hide even as he sought a broader audience. As Duke described his "awakening," research for his eighth-grade civics assignment had led him to the Citizens' Council library in downtown New Orleans on Carondolet Street. At the age of thirteen, he was captured by the arguments of Yankee segregationist Carleton Putnam's *Race and Reason,* and he began a lifetime of racialist reading. The writings of Arthur Jensen, Nobel laureate William Shockley, and other noted scientists added support for Duke's great discovery of the reality of race. The evolutionary process, he came to believe, had produced profound differences in physical traits, intelligence, and social behavior. From this came differences in racial giftedness, mental retardation, permissiveness and aggressiveness, size of sexual features, proneness to sexually transmitted diseases, need for instant gratification, cultural achievement, and racial patterns of illegitimacy and criminality.

Race explained everything. "Racial dynamics," he wrote, "constituted the essence of both mankind's history and future." Out of the European genes had come the people who had created American society. Now, with a nonsustaining birthrate and "inundated by massive immigration and proliferating non-European genes," America was facing racial suicide.

On Carondolet Street, Duke also learned that Communism was Jewish. His study of Judaism did not take him into the "Satanic couplings in the Garden of Eden" theology of the rising new Christian Identity churches, but he found it easy to believe that the Jews were behind the Civil Rights movement. The struggle was not really about civil rights but about Jewish drives for power. Judaism, Duke came to believe, was based on what he labeled "genetic exclusionism" and "supremacism." With what seemed like a shoebox full of three- by five-inch cards of facts and quotations, ranging from the Bible and the Talmud to newsmagazines, history books, and the writings of anti-Semitic extremists Edwards Fields and William L. Pierce, Duke argued that the Jews were loyal only to their own kind and were deliberately undermining America's European roots and culture. Through control of the media, they hid what was going on from white Americans. Illustrating this in a parable, Duke told the story of *New York Times* editorial page chief A. M. Rosenthal accompanying Texas Rangers patrolling the Rio Grande. In the middle of their search for illegal aliens, Rosenthal realized, as he described it, "I am one of them, the wetbacks, and not of them, the hunters." Rosenthal's loyalties, Duke went on, were not with those who wanted to preserve the American way of life but rather with the aliens who were changing it.

After college, Duke became serious about the Klan. Rising quickly through the local ranks, he soon had a Klan of his own. His attempt to appeal to a more educated middle-class America required that he live a divided life. While other Klan salesmen could freely offer their rural audiences the "nigger and Jew" litany that pervaded the world of Klandom, Duke had to take the path of reasonableness before the media and still manage to hold on to the traditional Klan constituency. This was a paradoxical situation, for none of the other Klan leaders was as deeply focused on the "Jewish menace" as Duke or as well read in history, the racial literature, and the story of Nazi Germany. Although all the various Klan leaders considered the root of the nation's problems to be a Jewish–Communist menace and were in touch with the various anti-Semitic groups on the Right, they considered Duke's Nazi fixation to be extreme.

Off camera, Duke was not to be "outniggered." On the platform, he had the orator's skill so generally lacking in the Klan world. In interviews and on television, he was poised, articulate, low key, and sincere. Tall, slim, and blond with razor-cut, blow-dried hair and stylish clothing, Duke's youthfulness and articulateness set him off from the rest. When he ran for the Louisiana Senate, he drew a respectable one-third of the votes. Was this a vote for the Klan? "Right wing," snapped the distinguished Louisiana State University historian and Huey Long biographer T. Harry Williams. "They got rich and are afraid of someone taking it away from them." To those who voted for him then, and when he ran again in the suburban New Orleans district in 1979, Duke was that nice young man who campaigned door to door and was opposed to busing, gun control, taxes, criminals, discrimination against white people, and all that regulation and interference from Washington.

Duke counted literally hundreds of radio and television appearances. A college speaking engagement might earn him more than $1,000 as well as a chance to spread his message and win converts. Only in his public television interview for a 1978 special, "The New Klan: Heritage of Hate," did he come a cropper. This time he was up against the *New York Times* star southern reporter Wayne King. Unlike most of Duke's other interviewers, King had the evidence:

> WAYNE KING: You sell things. You pass out things called "Nigger Huntin' License" . . .
>
> DAVID DUKE: No, we do not. I do not pass out—I do not . . .
>
> WAYNE KING: You do not, but your lieutenants do. Maybe you do. It came from Louis Beam.
>
> DAVID DUKE: Well, I don't . . .
>
> WAYNE KING: He's your grand dragon, isn't he?
>
> DAVID DUKE: No. He's a great titan.
>
> WAYNE KING: It says, "HAVING PAID THE LICENSE FEE (somebody's name) IS HEREBY LICENSED TO HUNT AND KILL NIGGERS," in caps, "DURING THE OPEN SEASON IN TEXAS." This is beautiful, David.
>
> DAVID DUKE: Well, it is a joke. Yes, it is satire.
>
> WAYNE KING: For a guy who says you don't belittle other races—I mean this is really pretty scurrilous stuff and pass yourself off as a New Klansman. Here's another one. There's very violent rhetoric in there, and some very—some of the alleged Jewish—"Ratstein" pictures of . . . who look like rats.
>
> DAVID DUKE: Now that, I think is excellent satire. . . .
>
> WAYNE KING: You really do?
>
> DAVID DUKE: It's humor.
>
> [In his calm, slow spoken way, Wayne King bored in.]
>
> WAYNE KING: [showing Duke a picture of a young man in a Nazi uniform holding a sign saying, "Gas the Chicago Seven"] You may remember this. That's you.
>
> DAVID DUKE: Yeah, that's me. Okay.
>
> WAYNE KING: That's amazing, David. "Gas the Chicago Seven"?
>
> DAVID DUKE: It's not amazing. I was young.
>
> WAYNE KING: You still sell the Nazi literature.
>
> DAVID DUKE: Well, I sell books on all sorts of subjects, but I don't sell Nazi literature as such.
>
> WAYNE KING: You don't?
>
> DAVID DUKE: No.
>
> WAYNE KING [showing a book list] *The Nameless War, Mein Kampf, Hitler Was My Friend, Germany's Hitler, The Testimony of Adolf Hitler.*

DAVID DUKE: Now, wait a second . . .
WAYNE KING: *The Hitler We Loved and Why, UFOs: Nazi's Secret*
    Weapon, My Part in Germany's Fight, Dr. Joseph Goebbels . . .
("The New Klan: Heritage of Hate," PTV Publications, broadcast
    by PBS television, November 19, 1978)

Duke complained that from a two-hour interview, the only portions used were brief selections that made him look bad.

Duke's media hosts and questioners on the networks were seldom as well prepared. Duke came across low keyed, thoughtful,
polite, and winning. His positions and philosophy held up, he
claimed, because they were informed and consistent. He had no
animosity toward any other race. He was only for the rights of
white people. The Chicanos had La Rasa, blacks had the National
Association for the Advancement of Colored People, and the Jews
had their organizations. No one ever complained about all-black
fraternities. He was not *against* black people. He was *for* white
people. Jesse Jackson and the Reverend Ralph Abernathy debated
him; Carl Rowan confronted him; Tom Snyder, Barbara Walters,
Jack Nelson, and scores of others interviewed him; *Oui* and *Playboy*
magazines profiled him; and Candice Bergen photographed him—
but none pressed him as King had done, and many found him sincere and impressive. Listeners phoned in, polls favored him, and his
mail grew. For a brief, seemingly incandescent moment, the Ku
Klux Klan had a star.

A historian who had come to interview Duke asked him,
"David, what is your plan for the future? The Klan is not going
anywhere. The Klan is a loser. Where do you want to be in five
years, in ten years from now?" Duke had obviously been thinking
along the same lines. A year later, in 1981, he publicly turned from
the Klan and founded a National Association for the Advancement
of White People (NAAWP). It was less than a graceful transition,
as Bill Wilkinson secretly taped and then made public the negotiations for the sale of Duke's Klan membership lists.

Now, at least formally, free of the Klan, whose mailbox he continued to share, he might be able to do better under the banner of
the NAAWP. His mind was set on the possibilities of electoral politics. In 1980, he had played with the idea of running for president.

Grand Dragon David Duke — 'charming,' feared and a 1980 presidential hopeful.

David Duke editorial cartoon in Fort Lauderdale Star-Sentinel, *December 17, 1978*

In 1988 on the steps of the Georgia capitol, with a National Social-ist campaign manager, before a small crowd that included Klan and National States Rights Party leaders, he opened his campaign for the Democratic nomination. Within a few months, Duke had switched parties and was running as the presidential candidate of Willis Carto's Populist Party. Carto was the founder of the Liberty Lobby, whose weekly *Spotlight* newspaper was read across the whole of the far Right. Carto had organized the Populist Party four years before as part of a white supremacist, anti-Semitic effort to break into the political system. Duke had attended conferences of the Institute for Historical Review, which Carto had organized to prove that the Holocaust had never happened. The Populist Party now provided Duke with funding and nationwide organization, helping him win 150,000 votes.

Having run for president as a Democrat and then as a populist in 1988, Duke now switched to the Republican Party to continue his never-ending campaign for office. He was narrowly elected to the Louisiana legislature and campaigned for the U.S. Senate twice, for governor of Louisiana, and twice in the Republican primaries for president.

Duke's initial and only victory came in the mostly white Metairie suburb of mostly black New Orleans. President George Bush and ex-President Ronald Reagan denounced him, the national Republican Party sought to separate itself from him, and the state Republican leaders remained silent. His fellow legislators did not take him seriously. He continued selling Nazi books from his legislative office and went off to a Populist Party convention in Chicago to tell skinheads and Nazis, at a closed session, that his victory in Louisiana was a victory for them and that they should follow his lead.

Within a year, the Republican Duke ran for the U.S. Senate in Louisiana against the conservative four-term Democratic incumbent J. Bennett Johnston. Although Senator Johnston won with 56 percent of the total, Duke captured 57 percent of the white voters. With statewide and national fame, he was now poised to run for governor. As a U.S. senator, Duke would have had a national platform and prestige, but standing alone in the Senate he would have been without power. As governor, he would be in charge of the administration of Louisiana, with its state bureaucracy, including the state police. It would be a measureless opportunity.

With memories of Huey and Earl Long in a state divided between the rich and the poor, black and white, and a Protestant north and the Catholic Cajun parishes of the south; the "big easy" city of New Orleans; oil, petrochemical, and utility industry political money; low-paying blue-collar jobs; a hard-pressed "forgotten" middle class that felt itself victimized; and a world of bottomless corruption and public cynicism, Louisiana was an opportunity threshold for a maverick politician.

State legislator, ex–National Socialist, and ex-Klansman Duke was now the best-known extremist in public life. His years of experience had taught him how to use the national media that rushed to report and exploit him. Soft spoken and affable, his Aryan face now enhanced by cosmetic surgery, he spoke to the cameras, not his questioners. New Orleans media consultant and critic Gary Esolen explained how Duke did it. Sure, he had done those things, Duke would say. He was young. It was a long time ago. That was not important now. Why would they not let him talk about the real issues? Why were they afraid of his message, about welfare and affirmative action, and how the white, European Christian culture was being dragged down by a black, government-favored under-class on your tax money?

Louisiana campaign law skipped over party primaries. There was just one big election in which anyone could run. If no one had a majority, there would be a runoff between the top two. Fresh from his senatorial campaign with total name recognition, Duke faced Edwin Edwards, who was seeking a comeback after three ear-lier, scandal-filled terms as governor. Although Duke was weak among more affluent conservative Republicans, he drew his major support from resentful white working- and middle-class Demo-crats. This was not a Klan or a hate vote; rather, as Tulane Univer-sity political scientist Lawrence Powell summed it up, "Duke's coded rhetoric" fed "a growing middle-class economic resentment that is not exclusive to Louisiana." Duke "had managed to rally an entire movement around the folklore that welfare spending is responsible for high taxes and blacks are taking jobs away from whites" (Gary Esolen, "More Than a Pretty Face: David Duke's Use of Television as a Political Tool," and Lawrence Powell, "Slouching toward Baton Rouge: The 1989 Legislative Election of David Duke," in Douglas Rose, ed., *The Emergence of David Duke and the Politics of Race*).

Again, the national talk shows gave Duke an easy ride, but he was pressed hard by more skilled newsmen and on *Meet the Press.* The intellectuals of the anti-Duke Louisiana Coalition Against Na-zism and Racism supplied the press and neighborhood canvassers with information, and Duke ran into trouble on the candidate fo-rums when questions were raised about his military service, tax re-cords, and anti-Semitism and his fumbling of the questions about his newly claimed evangelical Christian faith.

In a record voter turnout, Governor Edwards overwhelmed

Duke with 61 to 39 percent of the vote, 5 percent more than Senator Johnson's victory the year before. Duke had again carried a majority of the white voters, both Protestant and Catholic, and had done the best among the born-again and families with incomes below $50,000 a year. Of the 10,000 people who responded to Rush Limbaugh's nationwide phone-in poll on whom they would support if they could vote in Louisiana, 82 percent named Duke. His loss was not due to any surge of fondness for Edwards. Edwards's victory had come from an enormous black turnout and from a combination of upper-income and business groups that were disdainful of Duke and fearful that his election would mean racial unrest and would damage tourism and convention business and drive away new investment. The result can best be represented by two of the many bumper stickers that became popular during the campaign: "VOTE FOR THE LIZARD, NOT THE WIZARD" and "VOTE FOR THE CROOK. IT'S IMPORTANT!"

Although his perpetual campaign for office continued, never again did Duke soar so high. A perennial candidate in Republican primaries, he could not call on the lower-income white Democrats who had supported him in the open contests, but many expected him to run again for governor. The $150,000 paid for his supporter's list by the Republican Mike Foster, who did win the governorship, was believed to be a payoff for staying out of the race. However, the next year, Duke was again on the campaign trail, this time in the 1996 Republican presidential primaries. The campaign of Duke's fellow Republican hopeful, Patrick Buchanan, against welfare and affirmative action, with its disdain for African Americans, Jews, and immigrants, did not differ from Duke's, but Buchanan did not carry Duke's Nazi and Klan baggage. In Republican primaries across the South, including Louisiana, Buchanan pulled the votes of people who liked Duke's message but felt uneasy about the messenger. Buchanan, who always liked to batter someone, announced that he had come to Louisiana to bury Duke in the bayous, and he proceeded to do just that.

For those who stuck with Duke, there was no question about their racial beliefs. In 1999, Duke was again on the ballot, this time in a highly conservative white district just north of New Orleans. Republican Congressman Robert Livingston had been slated to be speaker of the U.S. House of Representatives until *Hustler* magazine let out the news about his extramarital doings. Livingston resigned from Congress, and in the open primary to replace him, Duke announced as a Republican. The national party leaders denounced him, but the Republican governor and state party chairman still remained silent. There were nine candidates, all conservative. Duke's 24,000 votes placed him in third with 19 percent, just out of the runoff. In commenting on the election, New Orleans University political scientist Susan Howell told the *New York Times* that "people over the years have asked me what percentage of the vote in Louisiana or in a district like the First is hard-core racist, and I never knew what to say. Now we know, and it's one out of five."

At the beginning of election year 2000, Duke sat as chairman of the Republican Party in St. Tammany Parish, the largest Republican parish in the state of Louisiana. His newest fund-raiser was the National Organization for European American Rights, or "NOFEAR," but while Duke was off meeting with anti-Semitic leaders in Russia, agents from the FBI, the Internal Revenue Service, and the Postal Inspection Service raided his home in search of evidence that he had been using white supremacist dollars in high-stakes gambling in Mississippi, Louisiana, and Nevada casinos.

· 16 ·

Klan Hunters: Morris Dees & the Southern Poverty Law Center

$\mathcal{M}$ontgomery, the capital of Alabama and the first capital of the Confederacy, is a strange place. The small brick Dexter Avenue Baptist Church, which was Martin Luther King Jr.'s first pastorate and home of the Montgomery bus boycott, sits at the foot of Capitol Hill in plain view of the governor's office in Alabama's monumental domed capitol building. Scattered among empty lots and single-story, motel-style lawyers' offices rise the gleaming towers of the Lumber Association, the Teachers Association, the Farm Bureau, and all of the other interests that tell you that this is indeed a state capital. A few blocks away on Washington Avenue, on a small slope, is the home of the Southern Poverty Law Center (hereafter the Center). The black granite memorial fountain in front was designed by Maya Lin, who also designed the National Vietnam Memorial in Washington, D.C. The fountain's waters flow down over the words that Martin Luther King Jr. had quoted from the Prophet Amos—"until justice rolls down like waters and righteousness like a mighty stream"—and then across names of men, women, and children who had died in the American civil rights struggle. The Center itself is state-of-the-art defensive concrete, steel, and electronics, for the Center is both hunter and hunted. The Center's investigations and lawsuits have played a major role in hastening the demise of the "fourth-era" Ku Klux Klan and cut deeply into the "fifth-era" white supremacist world. Striking back, Klansmen torched the Center's first headquarters, and the Center's creator and director, Morris Dees, heads the assassination lists of both fourth- and fifth-era extremists. Linger more than briefly

Civil Rights Memorial fountain

beside Maya Lin's fountain, and a security person will stroll over and begin a conversation.

The blond, blue-eyed son of an Alabama Baptist tenant farmer, Dees is a self-made millionaire who pioneered a legal assault that has shaken the white supremacist world. Using familiar tort law principles that make organizations and their leaders liable for the misdeeds of their representatives, Dees and his Southern Poverty Law Center have won multi-million-dollar suits against major Klans for murders and other crimes committed by members of their local chapters and added courtroom victories over major white supremacist organizations. In 1991, NBC told the story of his life in a television movie titled *Line of Fire*.

Through Dees's efforts, in 1987 an Alabama jury closed down the nation's oldest Klan empire, Robert Shelton's United Klans of America, with a $7 million dollar judgment for the mother of a young black man, Michael Donald, lynched by Klansmen from Mobile. In 1990, a Portland, Oregon, jury hit White Aryan Resistance leaders Tom Metzger and his son John with a $12.5 million penalty for the skinhead murder of an Ethiopian student. In 1998, with the Klansmen who had set fire to the Macedonia Baptist Church already in prison, a jury assessed $37.8 million in damages and punishment against the leader and members of South Carolina's Christian Knights of the Ku Klux Klan. The small rural black church and other victims and their families would never see much of the money, for the Klans had few assets, but the message was clear: "Hit them in the pocketbook," Dees had said. "Put them out of business." Pursuing the white supremacists into the new millennium, in 2000, Dees closed down the Hayden Lake compound of Aryan Nations patriarch Richard Butler with a $6.3 million judgment for the violent misbehavior of the compound's guards.

In other cases, the Center had gotten the federal courts to enjoin Klan harassment of Vietnamese fishermen in Galveston, Texas; closed down Klan paramilitary training camps in Texas, Alabama, and North Carolina; and successfully prosecuted Klan violence against black civil rights marches in Decatur, Alabama, and Forsyth County, Georgia. In yet another legal victory, the Center protected a victim's damage award money that the white supremacist World Church of the Creator, sought to divert to William Pierce's neo-Nazi National Alliance. All together, it was a punishing set of victories for Dees and the Southern Poverty Law Center that burned across the supremacist world.

As a boy, Dees worked in the fields alongside black people, whom his father taught him to respect. As a young, married student at the University of Alabama, he watched most of the civil rights struggle from the sidelines, though he tells the story of being removed from his Sunday school position for asking the congregation to pray for the children killed in Birmingham's 16th Street Baptist Church bombing. He came to resent society's racial prejudice and injustice and the privileges and racial meanness of wealthy white Alabama.

A real go-getter, he had organized a birthday-cake-delivery business for his fellow students at the University of Alabama, beginning a career from which he was to make millions in mail-order sales ventures and then use that skill in political and civil rights fund-raising. In 1967, he was one of the national Junior Chamber of Commerce's "Outstanding Young Men in America." Using his know-how, he raised more millions for the presidential campaigns of George McGovern, Jimmy Carter, Ted Kennedy, and Gary Hart, but his compelling interest was in the law.

Forming a partnership with Millard Fuller, a fellow Alabama law school graduate who was later to found the Habitat for Humanity program for building homes for the poor, Dees represented the American Civil Liberties Union (ACLU) in cases dealing with free speech, rights of women and minorities, and the death penalty. In a case that brought him bitter criticism from Montgomery's elite, he forced the desegregation of the YMCA, which had become the city's device to avoid integrating swimming pools and other recreational facilities.

In 1971, Dees and a like-minded lawyer, Joe Levin, incorporated the nonprofit, tax-exempt Southern Poverty Law Center. With presidential candidate George McGovern's contributors list and Dees's mail solicitation skills, they built a staff of investigators and litigators to back up Dees. Civil rights veterans Julian Bond, John Lewis, Charles Evers, and Fannie Lou Hamer; ACLU counsel Charles Morgan; Stanford law professor Tony Amsterdam; and newspaper editor Hodding Carter III have served on the board or as advisers.

The Center sued to integrate Alabama's state police, open up jury selection, and reapportion the state legislature. It took on capital cases of black defendants, including that of Joan Little, accused of killing a jailer whom she claimed had attempted to rape her in her cell. When the jury found her innocent, she thanked Dees and the other lawyer who had helped her by denouncing them as exploitative white lawyers.

Dees and the Center soon found themselves facing off with the hooded empire. Crucial to the Center's history was the violent disruption of the 1979 black protest march in Decatur, Alabama, by members of Bill Wilkinson's "Invisible Empire" Klan. The FBI initially failed to find evidence of deliberate plotting to attack the marchers. It took a decade-long effort by the Center's investigators to produce civil damages, jail for some, and a civil rights seminar for others. To accomplish this, an appeals court had to overrule and then replace a Reagan-appointed federal judge so that the Center's evidence could be used.

Decatur led the Center to set up "Klanwatch" to monitor and take legal action against the Klan. Dees and some of his leading investigators came out of the same world that traditionally fed recruits into the Klan, and they knew how to talk to them and to the juries of their peers. Sometimes, Klansmen experienced remorse. Sometimes, unable to pay for a lawyer, Klansmen found it easier to offer testimony in exchange for clemency. Sometimes, they threatened to get even with Dees and the Center. Backing up the skill of Dees and his courtroom litigators were Randall Williams, Bill Stanton, Danny Welch, and the other Center investigators who took to the back roads of the South to identify witnesses and gather evidence. With probably the nation's largest archive on Klan and other hate-group activities, Klanwatch has provided data to the FBI; the Bureau of Alcohol, Tobacco, and Firearms; the Justice Department; and Congress and has exchanged information with state and local police departments.

In addition to the circulation of its regular *SPLC Report* newspaper, its *Intelligence Report* has grown into a glossy quarterly that is distributed to police agencies around the country. Its "Teaching Tolerance" films, magazines, and packets are widely distributed to schools and teachers. Three of documentary filmmaker Charles Guggenheim's films for the Center—*The Klan: A Legacy of Hate in America* (1983), *A Time for Justice* (1995), and *The Shadow of Hate* (1996)—have been Academy Award winners or nominees. Despite pressure by the Center, the Klan world hangs on. Klansmen continue to be capable of violent outbursts, but, lacking in leadership, resources, and skilled legal counsel, they are pressed hard.

To fund Klanwatch and the Center's other activities, Dees used his well-honed skills to organize an impressive fund-raising machine. A steady stream of warning letters, reports, publications, photographs of victims and armed Klansmen, and solicitations, often signed by national figures such as George McGovern and Senator Ted Kennedy, brought the funds that built and sustained the Center. Above operating expenses, a growing endowment that many a college might well have envied reached over $100 million.

When the original Center buildings were torched in 1983, pictures of the smoldering ruins went out to potential contributors. As anti-Semitism intensified within the Klan and its fifth-era allies, the Center targeted solicitations to Jewish contributors.

The staff remains small, generally five litigators and less than a hundred supporting investigators, paralegals, researchers, educational and publishing specialists, and other staff, with increasing effort and funds going into the highly successful "Teaching Tolerance" program. Longtime Center workers mix with young interns and legal fellows from top national universities and law schools. The very success of its fund-raising and the battles with the Klan produced dissension within the Center in the early days. Attorneys and other members of the staff believed that the campaign against the now crippled Klan did not warrant the concentration of Center resources at the expense of other civil rights, poverty, and death penalty litigation.

At the core of the controversy is Dees himself, as hard to live with as to face across a courtroom. He is a brilliant, imaginative, compulsive, driving man, for whom winning means taking risks. Dees is the center of the Center. Being associated with him is exciting. Both he and the people who work with him feel deeply about the causes for which they fight. People both trusted Dees and felt used by him. Marriages did not last; coworkers disagreed and departed. In the mid-1980s, much of the legal staff and the chief investigator resigned, but with replacements, the successes of the Center continue. Victories closed out the Donald, Decatur, Metzger, Forsyth, World Church of the Creator and National Alliance, and Aryan Nations cases. The Klansmen who had set fire to the Center's original offices and the North Carolina White Patriot Party members who were trying to buy a rocket to blow up the new Center went to prison. With its financial success, the Center helps lawyers and advocacy groups in death penalty, civil rights, and poverty cases.

In February 1994, the *Montgomery Advertiser* published the results of a two-year investigation of Dees and the Center. For eight days, the *Advertiser* ran its story, with front-page headlines and pictures, entire pages on the inside, eye-catching graphics, and occasional foreboding editorials. Whether it was lingering elite resentment over the YMCA case or the required negative cast of investigative journalism, the tone was heavily critical. Along with Dees's success story and the Center's accomplishments came a steady drumbeat of criticism. In addition to the internal conflict over the Center's Klan emphasis and staff departures, there was Dees's imperviousness, salesmanship, and hyperbole. The *Advertiser* complained that there were not enough African Americans in top jobs and leadership positions, that Dees's friends filled the board, that he had offended the civil rights community in lobbying for the appointment of a pro–death penalty federal judge, and particularly that he pushed his fund-raising too hard and too successfully, was too concerned with endowment, and refused to open up his financial records to the press. The two years of investigation brought no evidence of misbehavior and concluded weakly with the recommendation that nonprofit fund-raising needed to be more open and watched more carefully.

As he told the *Trial Lawyers Journal,* the Klans of the late 1990s were "very few and small," but there was still work to be done. Dees's interest, however, was turning elsewhere. "There's been a change in the racist, white supremacist, neo-Nazi-type individuals in this country. They've gone from the Klan into paramilitary and skinhead groups," he told the lawyers. Dees's campaign against the Klan had already involved him with the violent rising on the Right. After The Order's armored car robbery in Ukiah, California, its leader, Robert Mathews, had shared part of the loot with Texas Klansman Louis Beam and North Carolina's Glenn Miller. After The Order's 1984 murder of Denver radio talk show host Alan Berg, Dees's name moved up to the head of its assassination list. Mathews died in a shootout with the FBI on Whidbey Island, Washington, but plots against Dees's life continued. In the new fifth-era world, Louis Beam had joined the Aryan Nations at Richard Butler's Idaho compound, and in San Diego, Tom Metzger gave up the Klan and was recruiting skinheads for his White Aryan Resistance.

By the summer of 1994, the Southern Poverty Law Center was tracking the militia movement touched off by the siege at Ruby Ridge and the attack on the Waco, Texas, Branch Davidian compound. That October, Dees wrote to U.S. Attorney General Janet

Reno that he believed the growing involvement of white supremacists and other extremists in the growing militia movement was "a
recipe for disaster." Six months later, 168 people died when Timothy McVeigh's bomb exploded at the Alfred P. Murrah Federal
Building in Oklahoma City. Although it had brought no cases into
court, the Center's Militia Task Force was pursuing the expanding
militia movement with the same intensity that it had the Klan. The
"racist right," Dees wrote in his book *Gathering Storm: America's
Militia Threat,* had changed "from a disparate, fragmented group
of pesky—and at times dangerous—gadflies to a serious, armed,
political challenge to the state itself." In the Klanwatch/Militia
Task Force report the next year, *False Patriots: The Threat of Anti-
government Extremists* (1997), and in its fund-raising letters, the
Center quoted Militia of Montana spokesman Bob Fletcher's
warning: "Expect more bombs."

· 17 ·

Yesterday, Today, Forever:
Klansmen, Klanswomen, Terrorists,
& Loose Cannons

I was standing in the small crowd of spectators at a Ku Klux Klan rally outside Lake Butler in northern Florida. A young woman made her way across the field to where the grand titan, in his flowing robes, stood. She identified herself as a reporter for the *Bradford County Herald,* expertly flipped her notebook open, steadied it on top of her purse, and demanded, "Who are you, and what are you doing here?" In this chapter, I examine who the Klansmen and Klanswomen are—what they are still "doing here."

For many years, Raphael Ezekiel, a University of Michigan social psychologist, now at the Harvard School of Public Health, interviewed major Klan and white supremacist leaders and Detroit inner-city young Nazis. In *The Racist Mind: Portraits of American Neo-Nazis and Klansmen,* Ezekiel divided white racists into four categories: leaders, ordinary members, loose cannons, and potential terrorists, all joined by the belief in the centrality of race, the superiority of whites, and the thrill of violence. In employing this highly useful typology, I want to add "conspiracy" to the list of defining beliefs. It is conspiracy that explains to them why the world is as it is, why the virtuous white race is forced on the defensive, and who the enemies (and the enemies behind the enemies) are. It is conspiracy that is the wine into which many of them dip their own wafer of violence.

The high point in Klan membership after World War II was in the mid-1960s. The investigations of the House Un-American

145

Activities Committee, prompted by violence against civil rights workers in the Deep South, estimated that there were close to 17,000 Klansmen and Klanswomen, belonging to the 714 chapters, or klaverns, of fifteen different, competing Klans. According to the prime Klan-watching organizations, the Anti-Defamation League and the Southern Poverty Law Center, membership fell in the later 1960s and early 1970s, rose to about 11,000 during the brief "fourth-era" revival of the late 1970s, and leveled off to a "fifth era" of approximately 4,000 at the end of the century. Klansmen have always believed that thousands more secretly support their struggle.

At the end of the twentieth century, other active white supremacists included some 35,000 to 50,000 members of the Aryan Nations, Christian Identity, and Posse Comitatus; perhaps 3,000 to 4,000 skinheads; and 1,500 National Alliance neo-Nazis. More belonged to other racist groups, such as the White Aryan Resistance and the World Church of the Creator, with much sharing and movement in and out of organizations. Of an American population of 270 million, the organized racial supremacists numbered perhaps some 50,000, or less than one-twentieth of 1 percent of the population. They are a tiny but enduring part of American society, and they are significant way beyond their numbers.

Over the past half century, the class base of Klansmen and Klanswomen and their leaders has remained unchanged. Larry Payne testified that he joined the Klan to "get out of the house and drink some beer." Payne was a member of the newly formed Justice Knights in Chattanooga, Tennessee, led by William Church, whose father had headed the city's Dixie Klan in the 1950s. The wanna-be Klansman son was seeking to become part of Bill Wilkinson's "Invisible Empire." One night in April 1980, Church, Payne, and another Klansman drank some beer and lit a cross overlooking the black district of East Chattanooga. Then as they drove down East Ninth Street, they fired a shotgun out of the car window and lacerated five elderly black women with buckshot and flying glass. At their trial, the Klansmen claimed that they were just "good ol' boys" who had drunk too much beer and who had not intended to hit anyone. When an all-white jury let the shooter off with a nine-month sentence and acquitted Church and Payne, black Chattanooga erupted in three nights of rioting, causing widespread property damage and leading to nearly 200 arrests.

The Klansmen soon found themselves back in court under the Reconstruction-era Ku Klux Klan conspiracy law. In federal court this time, the New York–based Center for Constitutional Rights used attitudinal polling for jury selection and expert witnesses, including a historian, the Southern Poverty Law Center's top investigator, and a federal Bureau of Alcohol, Tobacco, and Firearms expert, to win a damage award and a class-action injunction against the Klan. The Center for Constitutional Rights offered its success as a model for fighting Klan intimidation and violence. The Southern Poverty Law Center had come up with an even more devastating method of attack.

In 1981, the members of the Mobile, Alabama, Klavern of Robert Shelton's United Klans murdered a nineteen-year-old black student. Behind it lay the inability of a Mobile jury to agree in the trial over the shooting of a white police officer. As sixty-four-year-old Grand Titan Bennie Jack Hays, Shelton's South Alabama leader, told his klavern, "If a black man can get away with killing a white man, we ought to be able to get away with killing a black man." Henry Francis Hays, Bennie's twenty-six-year-old son, and seventeen-year-old James "Tiger" Knowles went out hunting for a victim. Michael Donald was on his way to a gas station for a package of cigarettes. They kidnapped him at gunpoint, beat him into unconsciousness, pulled a hangman's noose tight, and, to make certain, cut his throat twice. After bringing Donald's body back to Bennie Hays's house to show off their deed, they left it dangling on a tree across the street. From his porch, the grand titan expressed approval. "That's a pretty picture. It's going to look nice. It is going to look good for the Klan," he said.

Despite the cross that Bennie Hays's son-in-law had lit in front of the courthouse, the Mobile police were strangely reluctant to believe that the Klan was involved in the murder. Eventually, with information from an informer, the FBI got a confession from Knowles. Testifying in exchange for escaping a death sentence, he explained in court that "it was done to show Klan strength in Alabama." The jury found Henry Francis Hays guilty of murder and recommended life without parole. The judge exercised his judicial right not to follow the jury recommendation and sentenced Hays to death.

Lawyer Morris Dees watched the trial in court and came up with the idea that was to prove so devastating to the Klan world. Suing in civil court, he made his first use of the argument that the Klan could be held financially responsible for the actions of its representatives. On behalf of Beulah Mae Donald, Michael's mother, Dees brought Imperial Wizard Shelton and the United Klans of America into court and convinced the all-white jury that Donald's killers had been carrying out Klan policy. The jury took only four hours to award Donald's mother a seven-million-dollar judgment against the Mobile Klan members and the United Klans of America.

Bennie Hays and another Klansman went to jail. Lawyer Dees then turned his attention to the collection of the judgment. In 1987, the headquarters of the United Klans of America, a single-story, 7,400-square-foot building at the end of a dirt road outside Tuscaloosa, Alabama, went on the block. America's largest and oldest Klan—whose members had beaten the "freedom riders" on the streets of Alabama, bombed Birmingham's 16th Street Baptist Church, and gunned down Lemuel Penn on a highway outside Athens, Georgia, and Viola Liuzzo after the Selma-to-Montgomery march—and Imperial Wizard Shelton were out of business.

Some ordinary Klansmen, such as "Dynamite Bob" Chambliss, who planted the bomb at the 16th Street Baptist Church, were longtime members. Some, such as Henry Francis Hays and Chattanooga would-be Klan leader William Church, had daddies who were "kluxers," and some, such as Larry Payne, just wanted to "get out of the house and drink some beer." The ordinary Klansmen have been blue-collar whites, looking for belonging in a world that offered them little recognition and material reward. Particularly in the South, they come from a hard-drinking world that accepts aggressiveness as a measure of honor. Race is paramount. Black people are dehumanized, hated, and despised. Boundaries are all-important to self-definition. The Klansman knows that, however mean his condition is in the eyes of a more affluent society, he has heroic worth because he is not black. Because the black man is degraded and lacks worth, violence against him is acceptable.

Go to a Klan rally and listen to the responses of the faithful. Amid the denunciation of Communism, Jews, foreigners, and the national government, it is the appeal to race that stirs the supporters. The "Jewish conspiracy" is part of the rhetoric, but it resonates more within the leadership than the rank and file. The 1920s and 1930s role of the Klan as the enforcer of Prohibition and protector of the home and white moral behavior has long since disappeared. In a society in which the Klan can no longer enforce racial dominance or boundaries, "White power . . . white power!" is a defiant defensive cry.

But if the black man is degraded and inferior, why has the white man always been on the defensive—and never more than now? The answer is conspiracy. There is a sense of powerful enemies and the excitement of violence that has always clung to the image of the Klan. Although the hood and robes draw ridicule from others, for the Klansman they connect him with an honored tradition. They serve as a warning of the Klan militant to outsiders and an appeal for the recruitment of like-minded people.

The small-town Mississippi Klansmen who killed the three civil rights workers near Philadelphia, Mississippi, during the 1964 "freedom summer" included a deputy sheriff, three truck drivers, a farmer, a service station attendant, a used-car salesman, a bulldozer operator, a chemical plant worker, a former nightclub bouncer and trailer salesman, a Baptist preacher, and a mobile home park owner. The Georgia Klansmen who gunned down Lemuel Penn were a mechanic, a textile worker, and a gas station attendant. Viola Liuzzo's killer was a high school dropout and self-employed auto mechanic who had done time for petty larceny and malicious destruction of private property. In the car with him were a mechanist, a retired steelworker, and Tommy Rowe, the FBI's informant, a sometimes bartender, ambulance driver, laborer, and brawler.

Over the decades, the kind of people drawn to the Klan does not change. The Klansmen and Nazis tried for the 1979 killing of the Communist Workers Party leaders in Greensboro, North Carolina, included a tire salesman; a logger; construction, furniture factory, and textile workers; and a former Marine on medical disability. Except for the Birmingham Klansmen, most lived in small towns or rural areas, were school dropouts usually by the ninth or tenth grade, had theft records, were into second marriages, and were fathers of several children. Although some had been Klansmen for a while, most were recent joiners, shifting back and forth among Klans and Nazis, concerned about race mixing and Communism, seeking a bit of action.

In the mid-1960s, Alabama's attorney general told *Look* magazine that the Klan was "a channel for their frustrations" for school dropouts with a background of social and economic failure. By the 1990s, the oldest operating Klan was Thom Robb's Knights of the Ku Klux Klan, and the most active was Jeff Berry's new Indiana-based American Knights. The Klansmen whom Robb and Berry led through the streets of the Midwest reflected national demographics. Their education level was a little higher, but they still basically came from the blue-collar, mobile home, school dropout ranks, getting by week by week, worried about jobs, affirmative action, reverse discrimination, black crime, and unfulfilling lives. Membership in the Klan offers meaning and companionship.

For the most part, the leaders have continued to come from much the same class background. What the House Un-American Activities Committee had to say in 1967 about this leadership was not flattering, but it continues to hold true. The committee reported constant breakaways and reorganization and perpetual disagreement over aspirations for power, authority, and money. In the 1960s Deep South, a small proportion of the leaders "held positions of responsibility" in the general society: ministers, a chief of police, a municipal judge, a city engineer, a number of local business owners, and two members of the Mississippi state legislature. For the rest, the record was less impressive.

Half a dozen grand dragons were high school dropouts, and three had less-than-honorable discharges from the armed services. A Virginia grand dragon had been dismissed as an insurance agent for financial irregularities. A Mississippi grand dragon had been ousted by both the White Knights and the United Klans as well as a previous employer for theft of funds. Klan officials had records of grand larceny, aggravated sexual assault, burglary, theft, armed robbery, and other crimes.

For more than a quarter of a century, as others came and went, Robert Shelton, imperial wizard of the United Klans of America, which claimed branches in seventeen states, represented comparative stability. Discharged from the Army on a Korean War hardship disability and from the University of Alabama with failing grades, Shelton had shared the violent resistance to the civil rights revolution in the 1960s with Mississippi's Sam Bowers. The Klan provided an income and full-time employment for Shelton and his wife (who kept the books) and a number of his grand dragons. It paid for his Cadillac, his groceries, and his diamond ring. Like the wagon of an old-time traveling medicine show, his specially designed, one-of-a-kind executive camper opened up as a stage, with Shelton's rostrum and microphone surrounded by Klan flags, emblems, posters, and displays.

As Shelton stoically soldiered on through the 1970s, Klan fortunes fell to a low level. The various Klans were riddled with FBI informers, and the turnover of would-be leaders and followers was rapid and often weird. New Klan entrepreneurs, particularly in the North, had been active in the American Nazi Party and might even be Roman Catholic (before David Duke had officially opened up his ranks) and, on occasion, covertly Jewish.

In the mid-1970s, a new, dynamic, younger leadership briefly exploded into the languishing Klan world, only to find it too limited a vehicle for their ambitious martial dreams. David Duke, a committed National Socialist, was a history graduate from Tulane University, well read in racial social theory. Among the lieutenants whom he initially drew around him in his new Knights of the Ku Klux Klan, Alabama Grand Dragon Don Black was a University of Alabama history graduate, Louisiana Grand Dragon Bill Wilkinson was a former Navy nuclear submarine cryptographer, and Texas Grand Dragon Louis Beam had been a helicopter tail gunner in Vietnam. Some still fit the old, small-businessman, artisanal pattern. Ex-Army corporal and California Grand Dragon Tom Metzger was a television repairman. Arkansas Grand Dragon Thom Robb was a printer. Georgia's Dave Holland, who organized the Forsyth County march, built fences. Glenn Miller, who marched his renamed White Patriot Party through the streets of North Carolina, was an ex–Army Ranger and Vietnam veteran.

As a new image spokesman, Duke did well on the television interview and college speaker circuits, but this had its limits. Duke, Beam, and Metzger realized that the Klan was going nowhere, and, along with former insurance man and Republican fund-raiser Robert Miles, they left for leadership roles elsewhere in the racialist rising of the 1980s and 1990s. As Duke was testing electoral politics, Metzger and his son John were recruiting skinheads on the West Coast for his White Aryan Resistance, and Louis Beam was a rising light in the Aryan Nations in Idaho.

Bill Wilkinson, who remained with the Klan, was a better organizer than Duke, and his tough talk of guns and race brought a brief revival in the late 1970s. However, when the Nashville *Tennessean* revealed that he had been on the FBI payroll, his new Invisible Empire collapsed. With the others gone, Thom Robb inherited Duke's Knights and struggled on through the 1980s and 1990s.

The Klan was not going anywhere, but it endured. The pattern seemed fixed. At any one time, there would be some two score different Klans, each with anywhere from one to twenty chapters or klaverns, mainly in the South and the Midwest. They recruited their members through family, work, bar, or neighborhood; public rallies and marches; rowdy appearances on *Geraldo, Sally Jessy Raphael, Morton Downey, Montel,* or *Jerry Springer;* and websites.

Thom Robb was a bit of everything: John Bircher, anti-Semite, neo-Nazi, and Christian Identity pastor. Following Duke's pattern, he sought an improved public image, but he could not prevent the usual Klan breakaways. Marches in midwestern cities were not exciting enough, and he lost members when he tried to put hoods and robes aside. His main competition came out of Butler, Indiana. The Klansmen who signed up with Jeff Berry's new American Knights found their excitement in belonging, talking tough, chili in Berry's kitchen, armed sentry duty at cookouts and barbecues, confrontations (safely behind police lines), and the importance of dressing up in Klan regalia. As long as he would recruit members and share with the imperial wizard, almost anyone could become a grand dragon.

Berry's Indiana grand dragon was escaping from a dirty foundry job and life in a crowded trailer with an unappreciative, younger, second wife and the children from his first marriage. For the grand dragon of New York and New Jersey, with a clerical job upstate, it was a matter of pride and respect. It was exciting to invade New York City for a rally and be front-page news. In a *New York Times* interview, he explained the meaning of his grand dragon's robe. It was white like an ordinary knight's, "but it has three green stripes on the sleeves and a green cape on the back and a big dragon patch on the back, a Christian cross on the left chest, and a dragon on the right chest, and on the right side—I have to think— let me get my robes, otherwise I can't remember [then continuing] the right-hand sleeve has the American flag on top and POW/MIA flag underneath it. The left-hand sleeve has the Confederate flag on top. These are custom-made robes. We have special seamstresses to do this. They measure you for it" (Dan Barry, "You Don't Want the Colors to Run," *New York Times*, October 24, 1999).

And what about the ladies? There are no reports of Reconstruction-era Klanswomen. The mothers, wives, daughters, and sweethearts stayed home and sewed the robes. They did not, like the heroine in a Rita Mae Brown novel, cut their hair, bind their breasts, put on uniforms, and ride off to join the Confederate cavalry. Although Klansmen prided themselves for acting to protect the white womanhood of the South, when it came to black women, according to congressional testimony, Klansmen freely beat, sexually abused, raped (regardless of age), and killed black women and children.

In the revived Klan of the 1920s, women joined by the tens of thousands to be incorporated as the ladies' auxiliaries of the great fraternal lodge of white Protestant, native-born America. They organized its family picnics and youth activities; took part in its county fair days, ceremonials, weddings, baptisms, and church visitations; sang in its glee clubs; and marched with the men in well-drilled units down Pennsylvania Avenue in the great Klan parades in Washington, D.C., attired in their neatly tailored robes, capes, and pointed hoods. Half a century later, survivors told the sociologist Kathleen Blee, as she reported in *Women of the Klan: Racism and Gender in the 1920s,* how good spirited and community building it had all been.

Klanswomen also played a role in the Klan's dark side. Helping to act out its prejudices, they formed whispering squads, gossip networks, and "TWK" (Trade with a Klansman) boycotts of Jews and Roman Catholics. They sought to have Roman Catholic schoolteachers fired and campaigned for daily classroom readings from the King James Bible.

White Protestant morality was a complex mix of negative and positive values. The Klan's appeal was both fraternal and moral uplift. It came to town as a reformer, the militant arm of Protestant morality and enforcer of a dry America. Klan campaigns against vice, bootleggers, and corrupt city political machines and for better school funding as well as the Protestantization of the classroom attracted women from social lodges and church and civic groups, Prohibitionists, and other activists. Prohibition was an important Klan issue, and it had strong appeal among the Methodists. During the flush early days, the Klan meant the protection of home and family. The involvement of thousands of women and young people in Klan auxiliary organizations, Professor Blee concluded, helped normalize the Klan as "a part of ordinary white Protestant life."

Women contributed to the brief success of the Klan in the 1920s, and their history mirrored its downfall as well. Klanswomen were disillusioned by corruption and immorality within the Klan. As with the men's organizations, power struggles between the national Klan and state and local organizations helped destroy the women's Klans in almost every state. The great Klan of the 1920s had appealed to many women who had been active in their communities. Some of them had fought in the great Prohibition and women's suffrage campaigns, and others wanted to go further with a women's Equal Rights Amendment. The Klan drew political activists, particularly from the Republican Party. Never again would the Klan be able to reach into such a talented civic-minded, middle-class constituency.

As the Klan disappeared everywhere outside its diminished legions in the South, its role as family morality enforcer remained. In her study of the records of the 1920s Klan in Athens, Georgia, *Behind the Mask of Chivalry: The Making of the Second Ku Klux Klan,* historian Nancy MacLean described how women continually called on the Klan as a court of last resort to "straighten up" and punish errant husbands and misbehaving family members and neighbors. This role continued through the 1930s and in some rural and small-town areas of the South into the 1950s.

During the Klans' 1960s "third-era" resistance to the civil rights revolution in the South, the congressional investigators reported that Robert Shelton's United Klans had fifty-six women's units but did not report significant activity. So it was to remain. Various Klans have often integrated male and female members to fill their depleted ranks. There were a substantial number of women in David Duke's Knights. Some held office, and a martial arts–trained woman was chief of Duke's security guard. Women took part in the 1979 attack on the civil rights marchers in Decatur, Alabama, that launched Morris Dees and the Southern Poverty Law Center into their anti-Klan role.

There were no women leaders of Klans at the end of the twentieth century, and women seldom spoke at rallies despite women's websites and recruiters and estimates from qualified observers that perhaps as much as a quarter of the members of the Klan and other extremist groups are women. In 1999, when ABC presented "Women of Hate" on a *20/20* report, all they could find to interview was Klan leader Thom Robb's daughter, White Aryan Resistance chieftain Tom Metzger's daughter-in-law, and the daughter of a homophobic midwestern preacher. The Klan is a man's thing, and the Klanswomen are not drawn in by its ideology. Raised in it or being brought into it by their husbands or boyfriends, Klanswomen stand in the sacred circle, often with children in arms, the Klan's next generation, cutely dressed in miniature Klan robes.

With its legions so diminished and its resources and leadership so impoverished, why do we still pay so much attention to the Klan? Part of it is because the Klan plays such an important symbolic role in American culture and history. Its flowing robes, pointed hoods, and masks and its flaming crosses are the graphic and immediately recognizable symbol of prejudice, race conflict, and violence. They are the editorialist's and the cartoonist's delight. For African Americans, the Klan says it all. Everyone has a story. Malcolm X believed that Klansmen killed his father, crushed

Klan wife and mother, Davie, Florida.

his head, and left him to die on the trolley tracks in East Lansing, Michigan. Rosa Parks remembered sleeping on the floor beside her grandfather's rocking chair in Tuskegee, Alabama, as he kept an eye out for the Klan with a shotgun across his knees. For black people, the Klan represents both past oppression and what they are up against today. Even when there is no Klan, black people talk about the "klanishness" they face in the white world.

The other part is the Klan's continued capacity to do violence. By the end of the twentieth century, it might well have seemed that Klan violence would be a thing of the past. Justice was overtaking the last of the 1960s most highly publicized murders. The state courts of Mississippi had finally called the killers of Medgar Evers and Vernon Dahmer to account. For three decades, Myrlie Evers and Ellie Dahmer had campaigned for punishment of their husbands' killers. William Waller, later to be governor of Mississippi, twice tried Byron De La Beckwith for the ambush murder of Medgar Evers, state leader of the National Association for the Advancement of Colored People, but the all-white juries deadlocked. Then, in 1994, thirty years later, Bobby DeLaughter, a young white prosecutor, searched out the old records and evidence to try Beckwith again. With additional testimony, part of which the FBI had kept secret, an integrated jury found him guilty. In the Hollywood tradition, the movie *Ghosts of Mississippi* told of the struggles of the white prosecutor DeLaughter rather than the life of the black civil rights leader Evers.

Sam Bowers, imperial wizard of Mississippi's White Knights, spent six years in federal prison for ordering the killing of the three civil rights workers in Philadelphia, Mississippi. He had been tried in state and federal court for planning the murder of Vernon Dahmer, the storekeeper who was spearheading the voter registration campaign in Forrest County. As with the early trials of Byron De La Beckwith, the all-white jurors were overwhelmingly for conviction, but holdouts deadlocked the juries. This time, as with Beckwith, there were a committed young white prosecutor, an integrated jury, material now made available by the FBI (and in this case from the official 1960s state segregationist spy organization, the State Sovereignty Commission), and a changed racial environment. Klan witnesses testified that Beckwith and Bowers each had boasted of what they had done. "Don't worry," Bowers had said, "No jury in the state of Mississippi is going to convict a white man for killing a nigger." Now, in 1998, Bowers was not so confident, commenting that he did not have the influence he once had. On his conviction, the judge sentenced him to life in prison.

The same year, South Carolina executed a white man who had murdered a black woman and carved "KKK" into her body. The year before, the State of Alabama had executed Klansman Henry Francis Hays for the murder of Michael Donald. It was the first time in eighty-four years that Alabama had executed a white man for killing a black man. In a changing South, with strong black political clout and a new, young, white generation of law officers and prosecutors, old racial murders from the 1960s were being reexamined. Television's proliferating magazine journalists competed for the stories, with Connie Chung interviewing accused Mississippi Klansmen on *20/20* and a federal prosecutor reopening a case when an ABC News investigation discovered that the murder had taken place on federal land, where no statute of limitations applied.

Robert Chambliss, one of the bombers of Birmingham's 16th Street Baptist Church, had been convicted in 1977 and died in prison. There had not been enough evidence to try his confederates, but the memory and the wound remained open. Books were written. There was a black majority on the Birmingham City Council. In 1997, the filmmaker Spike Lee produced the documentary *4 Little Girls*. The new head of the FBI's Birmingham office told a group of black ministers that he was working through the files. With a state grand jury indictment and newly discovered tapes and testimony, the two surviving Klansmen, Tommy Blanton and Bobby Frank Cherry, were scheduled for trial. Bobby Frank Cherry was seventy-one years old, and the judge initially ruled that physical and mental ailments, described as "vascular dementia," made him unable to stand trial.

Birmingham's U.S. Attorney Doug Jones, who had skipped law school classes a quarter of a century before to watch the Chambliss trial, handled the Blanton prosecution for Alabama. Using focus groups and a professional jury consultant who had also worked on the Beckwith and Bowers trials in Mississippi to understand community attitudes, the prosecution concentrated on the bombing of the church and the death of the children, not the Klan. As in the Chambliss trial, the prosecution had the testimony of the accused's family members. As former Alabama Attorney General Bill Baxley, who had prosecuted Chambliss, commented, abused wives and girlfriends were a "common thread" in Klan convictions. This time Alabama had something more. It had tapes. Quickly identifying Blanton as a suspect, the FBI had rented the apartment next door and installed a wiretap in Blanton's kitchen. More tapes had come from the car of a fellow Klansman, recruited by the FBI, with whom Blanton and Cherry liked to drive around town, often after a night of drinking, parking across the street across from the 16th Street Baptist Church.

"Ladies and Gentlemen," U.S. Attorney Jones began his case, "it's been a long time." Despite fading memories and the circumstantial evidence of the case, the jury quickly found Blanton guilty, and he was sentenced to four life terms in prison. "Justice delayed is still justice," Jones concluded.

Many did not agree. Former Alabama Attorney General Baxley, who had convicted Chambliss, was particularly angry. No one had ever told him about the tapes. It had taken him five years to get the evidence that had sent Chambliss to prison, and then only because Jack Nelson, *Los Angeles Times* Washington bureau chief, threatened to make public the FBI's refusal to cooperate. "Dynamite Bob" Chambliss had remained free for fourteen years before being convicted, Tommy Blanton for thirty-seven years. Of the remaining two bombers, one had died, and Bobby Frank Cherry was declared too infirm to be tried. Just as these recriminations against the FBI mounted, a storm blew up over the discovery of at least 3,000 pages of evidence that the FBI had failed to share with the attorneys of Timothy McVeigh, bomber of Alfred P. Murrah Federal Building in Oklahoma City.

That the last of the surviving bombers had never been called to account stuck in the craw of Birmingham's black community and the Jefferson County court system. After more court-ordered tests, it was decided that Cherry was mentally fit to stand trial. He "has been restored to competency," Circuit Court Judge James Garrett announced, and in May 2002, prosecutor Doug Jones was back in court again.

There were no witnesses to actually place Cherry on the scene of the bombing, but the prosecution made the most of his career of violence and his boasts about the bombing. Estranged family members testified, and there was crucial testimony of his involvement with the other bombers in the days leading up to it. With the large screen turned away from the view of family members sitting in the court, the jury looked at photographs of the mangled bodies of the young girls, saw a video of a dynamite explosion, and listened to tapes of Cherry and other Klansmen talking about churches, the FBI, and the making of bombs. The prosecutions sought to re-create the feeling of a segregated, violent 1960s Birmingham and the character of Cherry and his fellow Klansmen.

There was to be no room for the suspension of belief about what was going on and what Cherry and his friends actually did. The jurors, prosecutor Jones told them, needed to look at the overall picture shown by the evidence.

Cherry did not take the stand in his own defense. The prosecution had destroyed the alibi that he had been home that night, taking care of a cancer-sick wife and watching wrestling on television. His wife's cancer had not yet been diagnosed, and there had been no wrestling on television that night. Nevertheless, his attorney argued, the prosecution's case was too old, too circumstantial, and too flawed. Character witnesses, including his present wife and two grandsons, denied that he was a racist. The minister of the small, mixed, nondenominational church that Cherry had joined in 1977, about the time that the investigation was reopened, testified that he got along well with black members. Cherry was a segregationist in the 1960s, his attorney Mickey Johnson argued, but so was the State of Alabama, which held the same beliefs for which he was now being prosecuted.

The jury was composed of six white women, three black men, and three white men. In 1963, some of them must have been of the same age as the young girls who were killed in the bombing. Others had not yet been born. After nearly seven hours, the jury came in with a verdict of guilty, and the judge sentenced Cherry to life in prison without parole. "Today the people of the state of Alabama for the second time in about a year," Jones stated, "have proved that justice delayed does not have to be justice denied."

The last of 1963's 16th Street Baptist Church bombers was now in prison, and people talked of Birmingham having reached "closure." Some called for "healing and reconciliation." Others still felt the pain. Journalist Diane McWhorter, a daughter of Birmingham, had returned home to find out whether her father had been a Klansman and to write the story of the white elites for whom the Klan did the dirty work. Her 2002 Pulitzer Prize for *Carry Me Home: Birmingham, Alabama: The Climactic Battle of the Civil Rights Revolution* and her classic blond good looks made her a natural for television. "Closure," she told the camera, "is a cheap form of redemption."

At various times in its history, the Klan has been a social reformer and a rally for white Protestant nationalism. It has always been a fraternal lodge, and it has always traded in violence. The aura of violence has been its distinguishing nature and an important part of its appeal for its members. The high point of its organized terrorism was during Reconstruction after the Civil War, when its violence helped drive the freedmen and Republicans out of politics in the South. In the twentieth century, the revived Klan never did its violence on so broad a scale and with so clearly defined a purpose. Only where there had been a friend in power, such as Florida's Lake County Sheriff Willis McCall in the 1950s, could the Klan ride freely and terrorize both black and white.

In the 1960s, Robert Shelton's Klansmen confronted freedom riders in the streets of Alabama's cities, but he had no grander plans. His instructions to the Klan road patrollers, who hung on the flanks of the Selma-to-Montgomery march, was no more specific than "you know what to do." Viola Liuzzo turned out to be a target of opportunity. Only Sam Bowers's bombing frenzy in

Klan repeats King's Selma-to-Montgomery march.

southern Mississippi approached what seriously could be called a terrorist campaign. At the end of the century, if forty members belonged to a klavern or turned up for a rally, then it could be marked down as a success. For the most part, Klans were too poor in imagination and resources to do more than talk wildly, but this did not mean violence was absent. Being a Klansman meant being part of a gang culture where primal honor was proven in violence. Though less mindlessly violent than the skinheads, in the Klan's obsessive racist atmosphere, there are always loose cannons.

It takes no more than two or three—or one—to spray paint Klan graffiti, yell racial slurs, make a threat, light a cross, damage property, burn a church, shoot up a home, assault a passerby or an interracial couple, ambush a black man, or drag a chained victim with a pickup truck. There is little likelihood that the Klan will ever again gain any of the tacit elite support or permissiveness that in the past gave it periods of local immunity. Even so, there will always be Klans as long as a would-be entrepreneur will appeal to the old mystique and gather a group of blue-collar friends to drink beer, talk about guns and race, and "doing somethin'" about it.

· 18 ·

The "Fifth Era":
An Explosion on the Right

Coda: Patrick J. Buchanan

Since Thanksgiving Eve in 1916, when Colonel William J. Simmons lit his blazing cross atop Georgia's Stone Mountain and reinvented the Ku Klux Klan, the "Invisible Empire" has expanded and contracted, fractured, and endured. Since the death of Atlanta obstetrician Dr. Samuel Green in 1949, no one has been in charge at the top, but Klandom still has always been mostly an anarchy in which the local klaverns did whatever they wanted. Joined together only in name and reputation, the Klan's competing empires stumbled along as America's only enduring political terrorist movement.

Since the Klan's great days in the 1920s, there have always been other militants—Brown Shirts, Black Shirts, and Silver Shirts as well as Columbians, the National States Rights Party, Minutemen, Sentinels, and others—but the Klan remained the big show. However, this was changing. In the 1980s, in what Robert Miles—the bearded ex–grand dragon of the Michigan Klan; pastor of the Cohoctah, Michigan, Mountain Church of Jesus Christ; and Aryan Nations chaplain—called the "fifth era," a faltering and beset Klan found itself being shoved aside in an increasingly crowded and violent Right.

Tracking across the 1980s and 1990s, there emerged a loose, violent white supremacist network of cults, compounds, tax resisters, constitutionalists, churches, racists, nativists, anti-Semites,

Nazis, paramilitary training camps, posses, militias, survivalists, bombers, bank robbers, skinheads, and millennialists as well as the bedraggled and depleted legions of Klansmen and Klanswomen. Where the Klan had been violently preservationist, the boiling extremist cauldron at the end of the century was part anarchy and part revolution. With little creative energy of its own, the Klan fed on the beliefs of the white supremacist world. Klansmen read *Spotlight, The Turner Diaries,* and the jeremiads of the Church of Jesus Christ Christian; absorbed Christian Identity theology; and fed on supremacist nativism, anti-Semitism, and conspiratorial theory.

The paranoid nationalist pride out of which the great Klan had grown in the 1920s had lingered on, particularly in inland America, in the Midwest, across the Great Plains, and into the mountain West. Writing about the 1920s, John Higham, a historian of American nativism, described the insecurity within a rapidly changing society that was absorbing waves of new immigrants who were no longer of the old northern European stock. For many older stock Americans, Higham writes, "The great problem was . . . outsiders of all kinds, alien in blood and faith and heritage."

Now, half a century and another world war later, the pace had only quickened, and there were those who could not abide it. The national population, which had been 76 million in 1900 and 150 million in 1950, had grown to 276 million at the end of the century. The massive black migration to the cities and the civil rights struggles of the 1960s and after, as well as the growing flood of non-European immigrants, made race the basic subtext in American society and politics. For a small but angry portion of white America that believed that race determined behavior, culture, and destiny, it was the only text.

To a much larger part of the population, there were economic changes and pressures that made them sometimes accessible to the racialist explanation of their problems. Life at the top was great. The number of millionaires more than quadrupled. If you were the head of a great corporation, your income had soared to hundreds of times more than the wages you paid the men and women on your production line. For many working people, however, real wages declined, wives went to work to maintain family income, and production jobs disappeared across the Mexican border and overseas. The high crop prices that led farmers to borrow money and buy more land in the 1970s yielded to a depression in the 1980s that brought farm bankruptcies and foreclosures. There was uncertainty and real pain on the family farms both in the heartland and in the towns that depended on their business.

In his book *Bitter Harvest: The Birth of Paramilitary Terrorism in the Heartland,* North Dakota newsman James Corcoran described the ideological rage that exploded in the life of North Dakota wheat farmer Gordon Kahl, who killed two federal marshals in a roadblock shootout and later died in the fortified farmhouse of a fellow tax resister in the Ozarks. Kahl, Corcoran writes, "believed that the government, manipulated by the Jews through the Internal Revenue Service, the federal courts, and the Federal Reserve Board, with the support of minorities, communists, and eastern banking interests, had conspired to take from him and his fellow believers, their farms, their land, and their way of life." Under the burden of his struggles, Kahl had become part of much that was percolating on the Right. He was a tax resister; a member of the Posse Comitatus, which refused to recognize any authority higher than the county sheriff; and a Christian Identity believer, and he had been willing to defend his beliefs with his life.

An important part of America has been the conviction that it is something different and better, an escape from the evils of the Old World. According to the racial version, those who came here first—Anglo-Saxons, Danes, Celts, and Germans (Nordic peoples, according to late nineteenth-century racial thinking)—were of a particular virtue. It was they who had built the nation. In the American heartland, American nationalism took on an isolationist hue. George Washington had said it in his Farewell Address: There should be no entangling alliances, foreign wars, and adventures, and Europe should stay out of our affairs and we out of theirs.

America was a great escape story, relived on the frontier—a world of individualism, open land, forests and mountains, far from the Old World, distant from the intrigues of government in Washington, D.C., and from New York, the city of bankers, immigrants, and, after World War II, the internationalism of the United Nations, the Rockefeller's Council on Foreign Relations, the

Bilderbergers and Trilateral Commission conspiracies, and the New World Order.

Amid the millions of law-abiding citizens of the heartlands, the fifth-era rebels, rejectionists, separatists, and revolutionaries planned their paths. Here on the Great Plains, the Posse Comitatus was born, and in the 1980s, a reborn racist Populist Party, financed by Willis Carto's Liberty Lobby, agitated among embittered farmers. Here in Idaho, Richard Butler planted his Aryan Nations compound at Hayden Lake, and Randy Weaver built his cabin on Ruby Ridge. Survivalists could "go off the grid" by themselves or retreat to the fortified Christian Identity compound, Zarephath-Horeb, in the Ozarks (renamed CSA for "the Covenant, the Sword, and the Arm of the Lord") or to Elohim City on the Arkansas–Oklahoma border. Robert Jay Mathews drew his Silent Brotherhood around him in the hills of eastern Washington. While David Lane served his 150-year sentence for the murder of the Denver radio talk show host, his wife Katja ran the Wotansvolk-14 Word Press (named for Lane's fourteen-word slogan—"We Must Secure the Existence of Our People and a Future for White Children"—which the movement adopted as its own) out of St. Maries, Idaho. It was in Colorado's Estes Park that Christian Identity Pastor Pete Peters called the militants together for the "Rocky Mountain Rendezvous," which birthed the modern militia movement. In Montana, John Trochmann lectured to the Militia of Montana about the "one-world conspiracy" of the Jewish bankers, and the Unabomber built his lonely cabin.

To the multilayered fifth-era racialist world of the 1980s and 1990s, the great evil was the federal government, run by an international Jewish conspiracy. William Pierce's murderous 1978 novel *The Turner Diaries* gave the enemy the name of "ZOG" (Zionist Occupational Government). This was the message preached from Christian Identity pulpits, carried across the racialist Right in the Liberty Lobby's weekly *Spotlight,* and repeated at Aryan Nations gatherings and at neo-Nazi, Posse Comitatus, Populist, Patriot, and Klan rallies.

It might seem unlikely that the growth of violent extremism should have take place in the 1980s. Even for those on the far Right but still within the American political system, there must have been some satisfaction or hope from seeing Ronald Reagan in the White House. Reagan had begun his presidential campaign in the South with a "states' rights" speech at the Neshoba County Fair in Philadelphia, Mississippi, the otherwise obscure small town of 6,000 people whose only claim to significance was the death of the three young civil rights workers at the hands of the Klan. President Reagan denounced Russian Communism's "evil empire," boosted military spending and a "star wars" missile defense system, pushed for a tax cut, and attempted to rein in the regulatory agencies. To run the nation's public land policy, he picked James Watts, an end-times anticonservationist, as secretary of the interior. That the Reagan presidency seemed to have no effect on the movement was an indication of how hermetically sealed are its dreams of race hate and Armageddon.

Robert Jay Mathews was ready to begin the revolution that Richard Butler and the Aryan Nations only talked about. Pierce's *Turner Diaries* was Mathews's model. He swore his small group of commandos into a *Bruders Schweigen* (Silent Brotherhood), sometimes calling it "The Order" after the Central Council in *The Turner Diaries*. Progressing from counterfeiting to robbery (first small shops and then banks and armored cars), in June 1984 they murdered Alan Berg, a brash Jewish Denver talk show host, who liked to make on-air fun of Klansmen and other racists. Next they took $3.8 million in a Brinks armored car ambush in Ukiah, California, and began preparing for attacks on dams, utility lines, and urban water systems. Mathews shared the money from the Brinks robbery across the racist network. First visiting Pastor Butler at the Hayden Lake compound, Mathews drove across the country giving large sums to Richard Miles in Michigan; to Klan leader Glenn Miller in North Carolina; to his hero, neo-Nazi William Pierce, author of *The Turner Diaries*, in Virginia; and to Klan leaders in Alabama. Brinks money also went to White Aryan Resistance leader and ex-Klansman Tom Metzger in San Diego and ex–Texas Klan leader Louis Beam, who was setting up the Aryan Nations computer bulletin board system.

According to *The Turner Diaries*, the next stage would be urban sabotage, but as the Silent Brotherhood planned the step-up to the new level, the FBI moved in. Helped by an informer and tracing the gun that Mathews had dropped in the Ukiah Brinks robbery, it rounded up the members of the Silent Brotherhood. Mathews escaped one trap but died in a flaming shootout with FBI SWAT teams on isolated Whidbey Island in Puget Sound, Washington. Two dozen members of the no-longer-silent Brotherhood stood trial in Seattle on charges of racketeering and conspiracy. Half of the accused gave evidence and pleaded guilty, and all went to prison for long terms. In a series of trials across the country, the government sent would-be terrorists to prison, including Glenn Miller, whose Carolina Knights had become the White Patriot Party, and survivalist James Ellison, after an FBI siege of his CSA compound.

Having invested major resources and with these successes behind it, the Justice Department now moved to strike boldly at the heart of the revolutionary white supremacist movement. Previous prosecutions had targeted individual organizations. With Operation Cleansweep, the Justice Department sought to tie them all together. Conspiracy has sometimes been called "the prosecutor's dream." The term "conspiracy" comes from the Latin word *conspirare,* meaning "to breathe together." In law, a group of people who have met together can all be held responsible for whatever crime one of them subsequently commits in carrying it out, if the prosecutor can convince a jury that they had been in on the planning. Thus, the Justice Department bundled an indictment of Aryan Nations leaders Richard Butler, Robert Miles, and Louis Beam together with already convicted members of Robert Jay Mathews's Silent Brotherhood and others who had been involved with tax resister and Posse Comitatus member Gordon Kahl and CSA terrorist Richard Wayne Snell, both of whom had killed Arkansas lawmen. Louis Beam eluded arrest for almost half a year and appeared on the FBI's "Ten Most Wanted" list before being captured in Mexico. In February 1988, all fourteen went on trial in Fort Smith, Arkansas, variously accused of seditious conspiracy for the forceful overthrow of the U.S. government through counterfeiting, robbery, sabotage, bombs, and the planned assassination of an FBI agent and a federal judge.

Butler, Miles, and Beam expected to be convicted, and not without good reason. While other white supremacists, including

Klansman Thom Robb, National States Rights Party leader Ed Fields, and White Aryan Resistance warlord Tom Metzger rallied outside the courthouse, the government set forth a pattern for violence hatched at Hayden Lake's 1983 Aryan World Congress. Crucial to the prosecution's case was the testimony of white supremacist leaders who were already serving long prison terms. In return for reduced sentences and entrance into the witness protection program, CSA leader James Ellison, his second in command, and White Patriot Party leader Glenn Miller outlined the plot in which The Order and the CSA compound were to be centers of the sabotage and terrorism.

The defendants denied being part of a violent conspiracy. They were racial separatists who had exercised their constitutional rights to freedom of speech and association, but no criminal undertakings had been discussed at Hayden Lake. It did seem unlikely that plans would have been hatched at such an open gathering, and the cross-examination of defense witnesses was not effective. Ellison and Miller came across as self-serving, and the government failed to convince the jury that the line between speech and action had been crossed. In Scottish law, there is a distinction in verdicts between innocence and charges "not proven." At least for the Fort Smith jury, charges were unusually difficult to prove. The judge had seated the jury in a single day and had not disqualified at least one juror who shared the same beliefs as the defendants. Two women jurors may have been even more difficult to convince. One of them married a defendant after the trial, and another might well have done the same had it not been for the long sentence that the object of her favor was already serving.

Although the Justice Department was not able to win its case in the Fort Smith trial, it was not wrong in its belief that the thread of conspiracy ran through the loose weave of the white supremacist world. In 1998, the Center for New Community, a faith-based organization that prepared church and community leaders to deal with hate groups, concluded that the line between legitimate far-Right politics and revolutionary terrorism had become increasingly blurred. The Center, which tracked far-Right organizations in the Midwest, summed up the white supremacists in four categories: "the biblically-based bigotry of Christian Identity, the

Constitutionalist racism and paramilitary organizing of Christian patriots, the hooded terror of the Ku Klux Klan, and the Hitler-worship of neo-Nazis and racist skinheads."

The soft face of white supremacy was the claim to be racialists rather than racists. They did not hate other races, but they loved their own white race. Their goal was not racial supremacy and dominance but racial separation in a territory of their own. What Robert Miles called the "10 percent solution" would be a white homeland in the Pacific Northwest, formed of parts of Washington, Oregon, Idaho, Montana, and Wyoming. To Pastor Richard Butler, this would-be Aryan nation was a "territorial imperative."

For all who might say otherwise, however, racial hatred lay at its heart, and in the fifth era, hatred of black people had been overshadowed by hatred of the Jew. In the tribal world of white supremacy, the crucial adhesive was a paranoid conviction of grandeur and persecution. The "Great Race" was under attack, and it was the struggle against these powerful malignant forces that gave the supremacist movement its meaning and its excitement. There was a great deal of testosterone invested in white supremacy, and the thrill of violence permeated the movement. Themselves a conspiracy, they saw themselves menaced by an epic conspiracy that only an inevitable race war could defeat. Christian Identity churches read the Book of Revelation and talked in biblical terms of end times, tribulation, and the great race war that must be fought before the Second Coming. Neo-Nazis dreamed of Hitler's Nuremberg rallies, Stuka dive-bombers, and the "final solution." Metzger's White Aryan Resistance and skinheads saw it being fought out in the nation's streets, and everyone read the description in Pierce's *Turner Diaries* of the "Day of the Rope," when Jews and race traitor white women who married or were living with blacks or Jews would be hanging from city trees and lampposts.

The history of the twentieth-century Klan has been a story of a struggle against imagined conspiracies. For the great Klan of the 1920s, a Protestant America was threatened by a Roman Catholicism in thralldom to the alien Roman pope. The historic outsiders, the Jews, were initially the object of less concern. By the end of the century, they had become the heart of supremacist demonology as the only conspiracy great enough to sustain its eschatology.

The Jew is the oldest conspiratorial fantasy of Christendom, complicit in the crucifixion of Christ, bearer of the Pauline curse and nearly two millennia of tales, rumors, and refusal—the perpetual other. Southern Jews had fought for the Confederacy, and some of them presumably rode with the first Klan during Reconstruction. The Jewish population in the South was small. Jews opened the dry-goods store on the square, lived quietly, and fitted in. The change of their image, in the South and in the American heartland, came with the turn-of-the-century growth of industrial and financial capitalism and the large-scale "new" immigration, which included several million Jews from Eastern Europe.

Faced with hard times during the farm depressions of the 1880s and 1890s, the western farmers were caught in a world of big banks, big railroads, and big corporations. Not without justification, small producers have nourished populist suspicions of those in the distant eastern cities who controlled prices and the money supply. Although banking was predominantly gentile, there were enough Jewish financiers, such as Jacob Schiff and Bernard Baruch, around to make suspicions plausible. Since its enactment in 1913, Woodrow Wilson's Federal Reserve System has been a major target of conspiratorialists, and the powerful European banking family of Rothschild has been seen as the heart of an international financial conspiracy. The face of the conspiracy grew. The Bolshevik Revolution, financed by a "crypto-Jew," John D. Rockefeller, and the spread of Communism were also Jewish.

The logical problems of reconciling banker–Bolshevik conspiracy theories have been simplified by the existence of a turn-of-the-century manuscript, forged by the police of czarist Russia. *The Protocols of the Learned Elders of Zion* was an alleged Jewish plan for world domination. No matter how often its authorship has been disputed, the story of Jewish conspiracy has been too useful to be given up, and it has been used to show how Jewish capitalists and Jewish Communists have conspired to dominate the world.

One crucial believer was Henry Ford, who found in it an explanation for all the things he disliked: big government, the growth of monopolies, the decline in family values, and, most of all, the big bankers who wanted to take over his company. In 1920, his *Dearborn Independent* newspaper, which was required reading for all

Ford dealers, used *The Protocols* in a crusade against what it claimed was Jewish control of the American economy, culture, and politics. In 1920, the articles were collected into a book, *The International Jew: The World's Foremost Problem,* which was widely distributed and translated into many other languages. In 1927, Ford was persuaded that his crusade was bad for his motorcar business. He denied knowing anything about the articles and closed down his newspaper, although, according to the historian of the old Christian Right, Leo Ribuffo, Ford continued to believe it. No one in America had done more to spread the belief in a Jewish conspiracy. At the end of the twentieth century, Christian Identity's widely read newspaper, the *Jubilee,* joined the game of picking the "Man of the Century." In its January 2000 issue, it announced that it was Ford. Eventually, Ford's grandson, Henry Ford II, was able to take control of the company from the old man by threatening to sell his and his mother's shares to the hated bankers.

The Protocols and *The International Jew* were standard fare for paramilitary organizers and radical fringe preachers. Across the Midwest, powerful evangelists Gerald B. Winrod and Gerald L. K. Smith warned against the international Jewish conspiracy. Winrod, known as "the Jayhawk Führer" because of his admiration for Hitler, carried the message in *The Defender,* which he published out of his Wichita, Kansas, tabernacle and in his radio message beamed out of Mexico when the U.S. networks refused to carry him.

No one could speak to the country folk as well as Smith, who eventually drifted into war against Communism and the Jews after the death of his hero, Huey Long. Encouraged by Henry Ford, Smith kept *The Protocols* and *The International Jew* in print and pounded out the message in his magazine *The Cross and the Flag.* In his old age, as his notoriety as America's leading anti-Semite declined, he focused his efforts on building the seven-story-high *Christ of the Ozarks* statue in Eureka Springs, Arkansas, and the production of a passion play in which the Jews could be held responsible for the death of Christ.

Buried near his towering statue in 1976, America's most famous anti-Semite had been involved in a dark world deeper than the traditional and now fading "Christ-killer" accusation, the crude pornographic images and cultural stereotypes, social rejection, and the belief in the capitalist–Communist conspiracies of the Learned Elders of Zion. Smith had had contact with the British Israelite movement through William Cameron, Henry Ford's spokesman and author of *The International Jew* articles. Having moved to California in the 1950s, Smith drew together the men who were turning a benign British Israelism into a fierce Jew-hating Christian Identity.

One of the mysteries of the ancient world is what happened to the "lost ten tribes of Israel," carried off by the Assyrians in the eighth century B.C.E. Differing theories have connected them with Ethiopia, Arabia, India, Persia, and America, most notably through the Mormons. In Victorian England, British Israelite theorists argued that the lost tribes had migrated across Europe and, as the conquering Anglo-Saxons, had made Englishmen the biblical inheritors of Israel's special destiny.

In the twentieth century, British Israelism was spread to Canada and the United States. As preached in Herbert W. Armstrong's great Worldwide Church of God's glass cathedral in Los Angeles, British Israelism was not hostile toward the Jews, but, in the hands of Gerald L. K. Smith's California friends, it was turned into a religion of hate. The racial gospel preached by Klansman Wesley Smith and Posse Comitatus organizer William Potter Gale took hold in extremist right-wing circles. British Israelism had become Christian Identity.

If the true inheritors of God's promise to Israel were the white Aryans, who were the Jews? As Identity theology evolved in the 1950s and 1960s, the "so-called Jews" were the product of either a mongrelized breed or, at the extreme, a satanic seed. At best, the Jews were a degenerative mix of other Mediterranean people. The ancient Hittites had provided the Semitic features, and the descendants of the Khazars, a people out of Asia who had converted in the seventh century A.D., became the Eastern European Jews. At worst, in the "two-seed" version, the Jews were the product of Satan's pre-Adamite coupling with Eve in the Garden of Eden. From Cain, born of the devil's seed, had come the people known as Jews, while blacks and other races were less than human "mud people," created out of the slime of the earth. With a heightened necessity brought on by the approaching end of the millennium, the Aryan people were faced with the struggle to save the world from a Satanic Jewish conspiracy. Setting down his prophetic Revelation while in exile on the island of Patmos off the shore of Asia Minor, St. John the Divine had written into Christian eschatology a warning against "the blasphemy of them which say they are Jews, and are not, but *are* the synagogue of Satan" (Rev. 2:9, 3:9). All told, with its apocalyptic vision of the great final battle of Armageddon, there was little of Jesus and much of Satan in Christian Identity.

Across the white supremacist world of the Aryan Nations, Posse Comitatus, survivalists, compounds, and klaverns, where Christian Identity doctrine was preached, the battle was already begun. From Wesley Swift's Church of Jesus Christ Christian in Lancaster, California, the Reverend Connie Lynch carried the message to the Klansmen battling civil rights marchers in St. Augustine, Florida, and stumped the segregationist South with his National States Rights Party ally J. B. Stoner. White Knight leader Sam Bowers listened to Wesley Smith's Christian Identity tapes in Mississippi. Bowers's bomber, Thomas Tarrants, growing up in Mobile, had heard Lynch and Stoner, and the schoolteacher Kathy Ainsworth, had listened to Swift's tapes in her roommate's Mississippi home. After Swift's death in 1970, Richard Butler, an aeronautical engineer whom Swift had ordained, left Los Angeles and in 1973 established his own Identity church and its Aryan Nations political arm in rural Idaho, where his Hayden Lake compound became the international meeting ground for white supremacists.

According to Pastor Butler's creed, the Aryan Nations is Christ's regathering of His people:

> WE BELIEVE that Adam, man of Genesis, is the placing of the White Race upon this earth. Not all races descended from Adam. Adam is the father of the White Race only. . . .
>
> WE BELIEVE that the true, literal children of the Bible are the twelve tribes of Israel, now scattered throughout the world and now known as Anglo-Saxon, Germanic, Teutonic, Scandinavian, Celtic peoples of the earth. . . .
>
> WE BELIEVE that there are literal children of Satan in the world today. These children are the descendants of Cain, who was a result of Eve's original sin, her physical seduction by Satan. We

know that because of this sin, there is a battle and a natural enmity between the children of Satan and the Children of The Most High God. . . .

WE BELIEVE that there is a battle being fought this day between the children of darkness (today known as Jews) and the children of light (God), the Aryan race, the true Israel of the Bible. (*Encyclopedia of White Power*, ed. Jeffrey Kaplan, 468–72)

This "revolutionary millenarian" anti-Semitism is not a Christian fundamentalist doctrine or belief. Fundamentalists generally accept the modern-day Jews as "people of the book," and leading preachers such as the Moral Majority's Jerry Falwell have been strongly supportive of the state of Israel. For them, it is the conversion, not the destruction of the Jews, that is to prepare the way for the Second Coming. In its anti-Semitism, Christian Identity has gone far afield from British Israelism's roots and finds no favor in the Mormon Church, which also traces its descent from ancient Israel.

Not all white supremacists have a theological turn of mind. During his campaign for governor of Louisiana, David Duke attempted to reap political benefit from religious conversion but could not remember what the name of his church was, and he did not show an interest in Christian Identity's feverish imaginings of "Satanic couplings" in the Garden of Eden. Tom Metzger briefly undertook an Identity ministry, but the skinheads whom he and his son John sought to recruit for his White Aryan Resistance were not generally interested. National Socialists and skinheads are more likely to deify Adolf Hitler and be atheists or converts to new jailhouse pagan sects, such as Odinism, created out of warlike Norse mythology. The youthful disciples of the antireligious World Church of the Creator are anti-Christian as well as antiblack and anti-Jewish. Many Identity believers, such as Pastor Butler, also greatly admire Hitler, but across most of the white supremacist world, Christian Identity has had the widest appeal. To conspiracy believers, it offers the greatest conspiracy ever told and brings religion into line by replacing Christian love and forgiveness with the call to racial war.

The leadership and followers of the racist rising come from a different class and background than that of the mainly southern blue-collar Klan. Geography and social location do not alone indicate any behavioral susceptibility. Millions who share the background—and often some of the prejudices of the Aryan Nations, Christian Identity, National Alliance, Posse Comitatus, and other militant groups—have not taken up the call. Almost everyone has at some time negatively personalized the forces shaping his life and society. For the militants, it is something more. They are seekers. A compelling search for answers finds it in one great answer: conspiracy. For the "patriots" of the Posse Comitatus and the militias, it is the federal government, responsible for the oppressions of the Internal Revenue Service; the FBI; the Bureau of Alcohol, Tobacco, and Firearms; the indifference of the Veterans Administration; the loan policies of the Department of Agriculture; and the fears of gun control. For the white supremacists, it is the Jew. For the militants, the two conspiracies—the Jews and the national government—increasingly merge.

Compared with the Klan, the initial leaders of the new racialist rebellion were older and better educated. American Nazi leader George Lincoln Rockwell attended Brown University, and *Turner Diaries* author William Pierce, who took over after Rockwell's death, had a doctorate and briefly taught physics at Oregon State University. Fellow Hitler admirer Willis Carto, founder of the Liberty Lobby whose *Spotlight* is read across the extremist Right, is a graduate of Denison University. Others also were college graduates, ministers, engineers, small businessmen, and retired military. They had been officers rather than enlisted men and veterans of World War II rather than Vietnam. William Gale, cofounder of the Posse Comitatus, had been a colonel on General McArthur's staff and had organized guerilla war against the Japanese in the Philippines. Aryan Nations founder Richard Butler served as an aeronautical engineer in India. Colonel Jack Mohr is a decorated veteran of both World War II and Korea.

An early step for many in their search for the answer was the John Birch Society. They were drawn to the society by fear of Communism, and it offered them the message of conspiracy. Carto and Pierce had been members, as were Gale, Minuteman founder Robert DePugh, and The Order leader Robert Mathews, but the

John Birch Society did not go far enough. It was not anti-Semitic and not rebellious enough.

Christian Identity fills the need for an overarching philosophy by combining conspiracy and religion, turning away from a confusing doctrine of humility and love for the hard face of Christianity. The Reverend Wesley Swift was a spellbinding preacher. Son of a fundamentalist minister, bodyguard and protégé of Gerald L. K. Smith, and onetime Klan recruiter, he introduced William Gale and Richard Butler to the joys of paramilitary organization and apocalyptic anti-Semitism. Out of the Christian Defense League and Christian Identity came the Posse Comitatus and the Aryan Nations. As the traditional elite anti-Semitism of college quotas, restricted real estate covenants and corporate hiring policies, and social exclusion were disappearing in the general society, a new kind was emerging. There is no report that Gale, Butler, and outstanding Posse Comitatus and Christian Identity ministers such as James Wickerstam and Pete Porter have had much contact with minorities, but blacks and Jews fill strongly felt eschatological and emotional needs.

Most of the followers have also had little experience with minorities. They do not, like the skinheads, live in an inner-city world characterized by broken homes, single parents, school dropouts, fast-food jobs, and dead ends. As the sociologist James Aho reports in his carefully researched study of the Christian patriots of Idaho, *Politics of Righteousness: Idaho's Christian Patriotism*, the militants were generally at least high school graduates, lower middle class, and drawn into various movements by the influence of parents, teachers, friends, coworkers, and pastors.

Robert Jay Mathews, the martyr–hero of white supremacy who had already launched his war against the United States before his death in a fiery shoot-out, grew up in a stable, supportive family in small-town Arizona. His father was a struggling small businessman who did not speak ill of minorities and argued against his son's growing rejectionism. Beginning as an anti-Communist teenage John Bircher and tax resister, Robert Mathews worked beyond that with the help of the National Alliance, *The Turner Diaries*, and Christian Identity at Pastor Butler's compound in Idaho.

To help get his revolution going, Mathews gathered a diverse

group together in the hills of eastern Washington and swore them
into his Silent Brotherhood. It was the relationship with Mathews
that carried them into his dream of an Aryan victory and bonded
them together. There were some angry loners, but mainly they
were family people with a lot of children, often into a second marriage, and not securely settled into job or career. There was a pre-
med student from Boise State University, a bright former seminarian from Florida, and two older students from Eastern Washington
University. Mainly, they were high school graduates, some with
good job skills. They included a construction engineer and electri-
cian, an industrial engineer who had lost his Boeing job but was a
skilled printer and with his wife became Mathews's counterfeiters,
and a storekeeper whom Mathews help set up in business. There
were a janitor from Philadelphia, fearful of black people; a rage-
filled neo-Nazi from Denver; a paramilitary training expert in need
of a full-time job; and a martial arms instructor. Only one member
of The Order had a prison record, a former AWOL Marine in for
burglary, a violent man who had learned about the Aryan Nations
in prison. None came from a settled life, and before Mathews drew
them together, most had already entered the racialist world
through tax protest, the Klan, the National Alliance, Christian
Identity, and particularly Aryan Nations—all told, a background
that made Mathews's passion seem reasonable.

Across the resurgent racialist world, white supremacy means
male supremacy. There is a substantial women's membership, but
despite rare exceptions and women-run websites, there are no real
roles for the independent, single woman in a hypermasculine
world. She can be wife or daughter but not "woman." Only
among the skinheads and in Metzger's White Aryan Resistance do
women play an active, sometimes leadership, sometimes violent
street-brawling part. In the more patriarchal precincts of Christian
Identity, Aryan Nations, and the National Alliance, the proper role
is to be supportive of their husbands and to produce, homeschool,
and raise white Aryan children. On the infrequent occasions when
a woman takes the pulpit in the supremacist world, it is as the wife
of a grand dragon or Identity minister. The widows of the racialist
heroes Gordon Kahl and Robert Mathews remarried within the
movement, and it was Debra Mathews's new husband and some-

times Aryan Nations compound guard who, in the summer of 1999, took his AR-15, his Uzi, and his Glock nine-millimeter to shoot up the Jewish Community Center in Los Angeles and kill a Filipino American postman.

While Christian Identity spread through the white supremacist movement and in small-town and rural churches in the Midwest and mountain states, there was an explosion on the Right that promised even greater opportunity. It was the combination of the government's siege of Ruby Ridge; the attack on the Branch Davidian compound in Waco, Texas; and the passage of the Brady gun control law that touched it off. Randy Weaver, a survivalist and a Christian Identity believer, refused to become a federal informant and failed to show up in court for the sale of an illegal sawed-off shotgun. An FBI siege of his cabin in the northern Idaho mountains resulted in the deaths of Weaver's wife and son and a federal marshal. Eventually, Weaver was tried, acquitted, and received a $3.1 million settlement from the government.

Six months later, in another bungled operation, agents from the Bureau of Alcohol, Tobacco, and Firearms raided the armed compound of an obscure Branch Davidian religious cult near Waco, Texas. Four agents were killed in an initial failed attack. On April 19, 1993, a fifty-one-day siege ended in a fiery conflagration in the compound that took the lives of more than eighty men, women, and children. The date of their death became sacred for the government haters and the new emerging militia movement, similar to the importance of Hitler's birthday for neo-Nazis and David Duke. It was on Hitler's birthday, April 20, six years later, that the two young killers would storm into Columbine High School in Littleton, Colorado.

After the Ruby Ridge siege, Identity Minister Pete Peters invited extremist leaders from around the country to a "rendezvous" in Colorado's Estes Park. At that weekend in October 1992, a loose alliance of the far Right agreed on a plan to fight against the governmental and New World Order conspiracy. The battle plan was what Klansman–Aryan Nations theorist Louis Beam called "leaderless resistance," the traditional cell form of underground preparation for guerrilla action. The new militia movement had been born.

The next year, the Brady gun control law, which banned certain kinds of assault rifles and required background checks for gun buyers, brought a whole new angry constituency into what its members call the Patriot Movement. Far exceeding the three million members of the politically potent National Rifle Association, vast numbers of Americans hunt, take target practice, collect guns, keep them for protection, and believe that the right to do so is guaranteed to them by the Second Amendment to the Constitution. There are few issues in the national life that produce such fierce proponents as does the "right to keep and bear arms." Convinced of a conspiracy to take away their guns and worse, a number of gun owners were becoming a conspiracy of their own. They were the "unorganized militia," sometimes composed of independent cell units that a malevolent government would have difficulty tracking down and controlling.

Like a prairie fire, militias formed across the United States, meeting to discuss government conspiracies and the black helicopters of the New World Order, gathering arms and munitions, and taking part in military field training and maneuvers. Despite the involvement of racial extremists in the Estes Park founding of the movement, the Patriot militias are not, for the most part, white supremacists. As Morris Dees, whose Southern Poverty Law Center (SPLC) tracked the movement, wrote in his *Gathering Storm: America's Militia Threat,* the militiamen are "mainly white and middle class. Most hold jobs, own homes, wear their hair short, don't use drugs," and "get a daily dose of anti-government venom from radio talk shows, respectable lobbying organizations, and even members of Congress." They are moved by "the fear of, and anger at a government that overregulates, overtaxes, and, at times, murders its citizens," a government that they believe threatens to violate the Constitution and take away people's right of self-protection.

As thousands of fearful and angry citizens joined the growing militias, Dees wrote to Attorney General Janet Reno that the SPLC "has confirmed the active involvement of a number of well-known white supremacists, Posse Comitatus, Identity Christians, and other extremist leaders and groups in the growing militia movement." Six months later, on April 19, 1995, the anniversary of the destruction of the Branch Davidian compound in Waco, Texas, following the recipe in his favorite book, *The Turner Diaries,* Timothy McVeigh—admirer of Hitler, hater of African Americans, reader of *Spotlight,* and sometimes militia attender—blew up the Alfred P. Murrah Federal Building in Oklahoma City, killing 168 people and wounding many more.

At the end of the twentieth century, the Patriot Movement was composed of a loose web of militias, Common-Law Courts, tax resisters, Liberty Lobby members, John Birchers, and other antigovernment organizations—without a hierarchical leadership or unified structure, reduced in numbers after Oklahoma City, and moving to the right. In addition to close to 500 Klan, Christian Identity, neo-Nazis, skinhead, black separatist, and other "hate groups," the SPLC listed more than 200 active Patriot groups. It was the absence of a clear racist commitment and the millennial call to war that separated the Patriot Movement from the white supremacist Right, but this seemed to be weakening. As the less committed dropped out, many of the remaining militiamen take a more extreme line. When Michigan leaders sought to offer a more moderate image—a "chamber of commerce with a Doberman," they called it—extremists forced them out.

The conspiratorialist world is an extremely busy one. Willis Carto's *Spotlight* and Christian Identity's *Jubilee* are basic reading. There are Patriot and supremacist journals and newsletters, shortwave and public access radio, and talk shows. In addition, almost every group has its own website, with the Klans and the neo-Nazis particularly active. If end times should be not yet, the Internet offers a possible new dimension. In the last part of the twentieth century, the old racism of Klan and anti-Semite and the suspicion of government experienced protean explosions in the form of Christian Identity and Aryan Nations, Posse Comitatus, and the militias of the Patriot Movement. In the new century, might the Internet provide a way to recruit a whole new cohort of would-be racists? Among the mounting millions of website hits are those of young people—rebellious, adventuresome, and susceptible—who otherwise would have been unreachable.

Teens and skinheads listen to supremacist music such as "Aggravated Assault" and "Stretched by the Rope" on CDs from

Resistance Records. People order movement tapes and videos off the Internet, read Tim LaHaye's *Left Behind* and other end-times books, and get together at gospel gatherings, music fests, Aryan fests, heritage festivals, and preparedness expos. Many believed that the government was deliberately planning a year-2000 crisis to stage an armed New World Order takeover. At preparedness expos, survivalists bought generators, purifiers, and rations and exchanged reports of the massing of Russian and UN troops already standing by in the United States.

Concern about the approaching millennium had not been the possession of survivalists and racists alone. For many mainstream Christians, there was a quickened interest in prophecy, which they shared with the Reverends Jerry Falwell, Pat Robertson, and Billy Graham and President Ronald Reagan. The quiet passing into the new century is not likely to have had much effect on dedicated millenarians and conspiratorialists. Failures of prophecy in the past have not necessarily changed the faithful. The time was not yet, but the intensity of belief would still hold. Although the postponement of Armageddon will not affect the anti-Semites, it remains to be seen whether a weakening sense of millennialism and prophetic immediacy might limit the spread of Christian Identity.

Within the racialist movement, it should have been time for a generational replacement, but that was not taking place. Gerald L. K. Smith and Wesley Swift had birthed Christian Identity in the 1950s and 1960s. In its second generation in the 1970s and 1980s, Richard A. Butler, William Potter Gale, and Robert Miles led it into becoming an armed territorial movement at war with the United States. With the reborn Populist Party, his Liberty Lobby's *Spotlight,* and his Institute for Historical Review, Willis A. Carto networked across the extremist Right, but the only forceful actor from the older generation was William Pierce, who had taken over an anemic American Nazi movement and given white supremacy a sacred fantasy in *The Turner Diaries.* In his sixties, Pierce selected young, active lieutenants with experience in youth and armed service underground organizing, strengthened his youth outreach with the purchase of Resistance Records (the prime producer of racist music), and worked on ties with Canadian and European neo-Nazi groups. In the summer of 2002, Pierce died of cancer at the age of sixty-nine. The second generation was gone, and there were no promising successors.

The activism of the 1980s and 1990s has brought an increasing response from state and national authorities. States and the federal government prosecute Freemen and Common-Law Court members for false liens and filings, fraud, and harassment of government officials. While most militia activity is aboveground, members are going to jail on domestic terrorism charges, including weapons and explosives, assault, and planned bomb plots and assassinations. Despite state laws upping the penalties for "hate crimes," Klan and skinhead street violence continues, and terrorist planning increases across the extremist underground. This, in turn, has brought rising attention from the FBI. Mark Potok, editor of the SPLC's newly expanded *Intelligence Report,* reported in the summer of 2001 that since the Oklahoma City bombing, the government has been able to prevent at least twenty-nine serious terrorist plots, including bombings of federal buildings and the Internal Revenue Service, attacks on armories, and assassinations of judges and federal officials.

For an American nation that will soon number 300 million people, the racialist Right seems too far out, too violent, too chaotic, too poor, and too lacking in leadership to become a political force. But how firm are the institutions and values that hold together a tolerant, multicultural America, particularly after the terrorist attacks of September 11? The racial and ethnic mix of America is rapidly changing. Is there the possibility of a rising ethnic nationalism and a reaction to Middle East terrorism on whose ragged edge the white supremacists can find a place?

The best test of whether there is enough anger in the country to fuel a movement was the pit-dog presidential candidacy of Patrick J. Buchanan. Buchanan was an established media celebrity and an intellectual spokesman for the right wing of the Republican party. He wrote speeches and planned dirty tricks for President Richard Nixon and liberal-bashing speeches for Vice President Spiro Agnew. He had been White House communications director for President Reagan. Buchanan believed that the mushy centrist Republicanism of the Robert Doles and George Bushes meant opportunity on the Right for a nationalist leader, and he was ready. He had fire in his belly, the oratorical skills, the contacts, and the public attention. Television talk shows *Crossfire* and *The McLaughlin Group* liked his brash, chuckling wit, and his role as lecturer, writer, and media personality made him independently wealthy.

Buchanan's politics combined an updated "America first" nationalism, the "cultural war" social philosophy of the religious Right, and a populist attack on big business and capitalist greed. To this, he added a belligerent nativism that shared many of the prejudices that drove the racial extremists, some of whom turned up in his political campaigns. If there was the possibility of building a mainstream following on the far-Right edge, it might come from the multi-million-dollar conspiracy-hawking campaign of movie celebrity Charlton Heston, president of the National Rifle Association, and the nationalist politics of Buchanan.

Buchanan made his first move at the 1992 Republican National Convention in Houston. To the dismay of the Republican establishment, he called for "a religious war" for the soul of America. As the Los Angeles police had taken back the streets "block by block" from the racial rioters, he proclaimed, "we must take back our cities, and take back our culture, and take back our country."

Four years later, in 1996, running for the Republican presidential nomination, Buchanan bested Senator Robert Dole, the eventual nominee, in the New Hampshire primary and took Louisiana away from David Duke.

In 1996, there were two masterful television performers: President William Jefferson Clinton and Patrick Buchanan. In the 2000 presidential election, there was only Buchanan, now in possession of the fractious remains of Ross Perot's Reform Party, with its $12 million of federal campaign financing.

Buchanan had grown up in a patriarchal "better Hitler than Stalin" family in which the Spanish dictator Francisco Franco and Senator Joseph McCarthy were household heroes. Buchanan's Jesuit-nurtured Catholicism did not disturb the conservative Christians who shared his support for the traditional family, school prayer and vouchers, and opposition to abortion, homosexuality, and multiculturalism. "Our culture is superior," Buchanan proclaimed, "because our religion is Christianity."

He condemned the United Nations and the globalist elites and their supernational organizations, the use of American troops as peacekeepers outside North America, foreign aid, the free-trade treaty with Canada and Mexico, special trade relations with China, and the immigrant flood of peoples from the non-European world. Immigration should be closed for five years, he proposed, and then reopened on a more limited, selective basis.

And there was something more, stepping close to, and some people felt over, the line that separated right-wing from racist politics. Although there is a difference between criticism of Israeli policy and anti-Semitism, Buchanan's repeated comments led many, including his onetime idol, conservative critic William F. Buckley, to call his comments anti-Semitic. His Holocaust-minimizing defense of accused Nazi war criminals, his praise of Hitler, and the words he wrote for President Reagan to speak over the SS dead in the Bitburg cemetery were treading on the edge.

With both Al Gore and George W. Bush and their parties crowding the political center, Buchanan saw the opening on the Right. Only a little more than half of the 200 million voting-age people in the United States ever bother to vote. A quarter of them are not even registered. In the 2000 election, Buchanan sought to offer a powerful alternative both for alienated conservatives and for those outside the political system. A surge for Buchanan could mean possibilities further to the Right. The excitement of a close election did draw a larger-than-usual vote for the centrist Democratic and Republican Parties. Gore and Bush each received some fifty-eight million votes, but there was no swell on the Right. Buchanan's share was 441,000 votes, or less than four-tenths of 1 percent. There was going to be no new mainstream rally on the far Right.

Without an infusion of political support or cover and the emergence of a new young leader or plan, the white supremacist insurrection stumbled on, anarchic and deadly. The second-generation leaders were aging or gone. The closest that Aryan Nations patriarch Richard Butler came to creating a white homeland out of the Pacific Northwest was his twenty-acre fortified Hayden Lake compound. Now, Morris Dees and the SPLC had taken it away from him—trophies, flags, bust of Hitler, everything. Militiamen were either getting tired and going home or getting into trouble and going to jail. Judges and juries were more likely to find Klansmen guilty and to increase the penalties. Former Aryan Nations leader Butler's guards went to prison, and he lost his Hayden Lake compound because the guards had harassed passersby, and American Knights leader Jeff Berry drew a seven-year prison term for similarly mistreating television journalists.

Although the twenty-first century did not give promise of mainstream acceptability or a compelling leadership and a unified movement, the ingredients of an economy of hate still fed a violent right wing. The soaring growth of a non-European population mix in the United States fueled an ethnic nationalism that believed that a white American civilization was under attack. The SPLC reported that the web of association between northern European fascists and American right-wing extremists was thickening. There were increasing ties with racial nationalists and neo-Nazis from England to Russia, where David Duke visited with the leaders and had a Russian translation of his autobiography.

The American mainstream may have breathed too easily when the world slipped out of the old millennium without an explosion. At the beginning of the twenty-first century, it threatened in the form of two geographically based apocalyptic populisms that rejected modern, open society. One connected racial nationalists of North America and Europe, and the other cut a radical Islamic swath across the Middle East. Each was prepared to defend violently a culture that it believed was under attack by outsiders. As the traditional expression of racial prejudice and violence in the United States, no matter how ragged and diminished the Klan was, it was not going to disappear.

Essay on Sources

$\mathcal{L}$eading spokesmen for the white supremacist movement have been *The Fiery Cross* (1960–1987), the official organ of Robert Shelton's United Klans of America, and David Duke's *The Crusader* (Metairie, La.), the Liberty Lobby's *Spotlight* (Washington, D.C.), and Christian Identity's *Jubilee* (Midpines, Calif.). *The Turner Diaries* (Washington, D.C., 1978), by neo-Nazi National Alliance Leader William Pierce (pen name Andrew Macdonald), provided the plan and the inspiration for Robert Mathews's The Order and the bombing of the Alfred P. Murrah Federal Building in Oklahoma City. The only personal writing to come out of the movement is David Duke's *My Awakening: A Path to Racial Understanding* (Mandeville, La.: Free Speech Press, 1998), in which Duke offered a serious argument on race, a heated condemnation of the Jews, and his own autobiography. Duke's favorite statement on the racial history of the United States is Humphrey Ireland's *The Dispossessed Majority* (Cape Canaveral, Fla.: Howard Allen, 1972), published under the pen name Wilmot Robertson. The Southern Poverty Law Center's *Intelligence Report* (Montgomery, Ala.) periodically publishes lists of white supremacist and patriot organizations and in its winter 1998 issue gives their Internet addresses.

The Ku Klux Klan: An Encyclopedia, edited by Milton and Judy Ann Newton (New York: Garland Publishing, 1991) is a highly useful reference work covering more than a hundred years of the Ku Klux Klan. The Anti-Defamation League's latest compilation, *Danger Extremism: The Major Vehicles and Voices on America's Far-Right Fringe* (New York: Anti-Defamation League, 1996), and Jeffrey Kaplan's excellent *Encyclopedia of White Power* (Walnut Creek, Calif.: AltaMira Press, 2000) serve the same function for the last quarter of the twentieth century. The best general account of the "fifth-era" extremists on the Right up to 1990 is James Ridgeway, *Blood in the Face: The Ku Klux Klan, Aryan Nations, Nazi Skinheads, and the Rise of a New White Culture* (New York: Thunder Mouth Press, 1990). Allen Trelease's *White Terror: The Ku Klux Klan and Southern Reconstruction* (New York: Harper & Row, 1971) is a magisterial history of the Reconstruction Klan. The standard history of the first four eras of the Klan is David Chalmers, *Hooded Americanism: The History of the Ku Klux Klan* (Durham, N.C.: Duke University Press, 1987).

When the Klan or other supremacist or patriot organizations or individuals make news, it can be traced through the *New York Times Index* and stories. Newsmagazine stories in *Time* and *Newsweek* and in the *Saturday Evening Post* and *Look* and other accounts and commentary can be traced through the *Reader's Guide to Periodical Literature*. Facts on File is useful, and for anything involving Congress, the *Congressional Quarterly Almanac* is outstanding. The Southern Regional Council's *New South,* succeeded by *Southern Changes* and the American Friends Service Committee, provides useful reports on southern violence.

Although they do not find anything favorable to say about it, the Anti-Defamation League, the Southern Poverty Law Center, the Center for Democratic Renewal, and, since 1994, the Center for New Community monitor extremism on the Right and are the prime source of reliable published information. Founded in 1913, the Anti-Defamation League, with headquarters in New York City and offices around the country, defends the rights of Jews and other minorities and regularly publishes books, in-depth studies, and reports on hate groups. The Southern Poverty Law Center (SPLC) was founded in 1971 and operates out of Montgomery, Alabama. In addition to investigation and litigation and providing "teaching tolerance" materials to schools and intelligence to police forces, the SPLC's *Intelligence Report,* now published quarterly, is the most extensive source of public information on right-wing extremism. The Center for Democratic Renewal in Atlanta, Georgia, grew out of the Anti-Klan Network founded by the Southern

Christian Leadership Conference after the 1979 killings in Greensboro, North Carolina. The Center for New Community (CNC), in Oak Park, Illinois, is a faith-based organization that makes reports, holds conferences, and helps Midwest communities organize against hate groups. The SPLC's special report "The Ku Klux Klan: A History of Racism and Violence" (3rd ed., 1988) and the CNC's "The Far-Right in the Midwest" (1999) are good starting points.

For the civil rights era, Numan Bartley's *The New South, 1945–1980* (Baton Rouge: Louisiana State University Press, 1995), in the History of the South series, is a reliable overview. *New York Times* man Howell Raines's *My Soul Is Rested: The Story of the Civil Rights Movement in the Deep South* (New York: Penguin, 1977) is an excellent oral history collection, although the selections are too brief. William Rogers, Robert Ward, Leah Atkins, and Wayne Flynt's *Alabama: The History of a Deep South State* (Tuscaloosa: University of Alabama Press, 1994) is the best of the state histories. Pulitzer Prize–winning historians Taylor Branch's *Parting the Waters: America in the King Years, 1954–1963* (New York: Simon & Schuster, 1988) and *Pillar of Fire: America in the King Years, 1963–65* (New York: Simon & Schuster, 1998) and David Garrow's *Bearing the Cross, Martin Luther King, Jr., and the Southern Christian Leadership Conference* (New York: Murrow, 1986) are marvels of research and oral history, as is Dan Carter's political biography of George Wallace, *The Politics of Rage: George Wallace, the Origins of the New Conservatism, and the Transformation of American Politics* (Baton Rouge: Louisiana State University Press, 1995). David Halberstam's *The Children* (New York: Random House, 1998) is the insightful biography of the Nashville contingent who were at the heart of the Student Nonviolent Coordinating Committee.

The struggles in most of the Deep South states have their outstanding historians. In Alabama, it is Glen Eskew, *But for Birmingham* (Chapel Hill: University of North Carolina Press, 1997). The stories of Klan victims are told in Mary Stanton's *From Selma to Sorrow: The Life and Death of Viola Liuzzo* (Athens: University of Georgia Press, 1998) and Frank Sikora's *Until Justice Rolls Down: The Birmingham Church Bombing Case* (Tuscaloosa:

University of Alabama Press, 1991). Diane McWhorter's Pulitzer Prize–winning *Carry Me Home: Birmingham, Alabama: The Climactic Battle of the Civil Rights Revolution* (New York: Simon & Schuster, 2001) is the story of a New York journalist who went home to Birmingham to investigate the connection between her class and family and the Klan. David Garrow offers an incisive review of the literature on Birmingham in "Many Birminghams: Taking Segregationists Seriously," *Southern Changes* 23, no. 2 (summer 2001): 26–32. For Florida, it is David Colburn, *Racial Change and Community Crisis: St. Augustine Florida, 1877–1980* (New York: Columbia University Press, 1985). For Mississippi, it is Seth Cagin and Philip Dray, *We Are Not Afraid: The Mississippi Murders of Goodman, Schwerner, and Chaney and the Civil Rights Campaign for Mississippi* (New York: Macmillan, 1988); John Dittmer, *Local People: The Struggle for Civil Rights in Mississippi* (Urbana: University of Illinois Press, 1944); and Jack Nelson, *Terror in the Night: The Klan's Campaign against the Jews* (New York: Simon & Schuster, 1970). The essay on Mississippi White Knight Sam Bowers in Charles Marsh, *God's Long Summer: Stories of Faith and Civil Rights* (Princeton, N.J.: Princeton University Press, 1997), is an exception to the lack of treatment of Klan leaders. Adam Fairclough's *Race and Democracy: The Civil Rights Struggle in Louisiana, 1915–1972* (Athens: University of Georgia Press, 1995), tells the Louisiana story. Clive Webb's *Fight against Fear: Southern Jews and Black Civil Rights* (Athens: University of Georgia Press, 2001), impressive in its broad coverage, tells of how, despite a general self-protective silence, the activities of a minority of women and rabbis tagged the Jews as a threat to white solidarity without winning the appreciation of the black nationalists.

The role of the federal government is treated in Michal Belknap's outstanding *Federal Law and Southern Order: Racial Violence and Constitutional Conflict in the Post-Brown South* (Athens: University of Georgia Press, 1987); in Jack Bass, *Taming the Storm: The Life and Times of Judge Frank M. Johnson, Jr., and the South's Fight over Civil Rights* (New York: Doubleday, 1993); and, not favorably, in Kenneth O'Reilly, *"Racial Matters": The FBI's Secret File on Black America, 1960–1972* (New York: Free Press, 1989), and Victor Navasky, *Kennedy Justice* (New York: Atheneum,

1971). To almost everyone's surprise, the House Un-American Activities Committee conducted a serious and informative investigation, "Activities of Ku Klux Klan Organizations in the United States," Hearings, Report, Contempt Citations, Bills, 1965–1967. The U.S. Senate Select Committee on Intelligence Activities (1975) Hearings on the FBI (Vol. 5) and its Final Report deal critically with the federal government.

For the "fourth era" of the Klans in the 1970s and 1980s, Elizabeth Wheaton's *Codename Greenkill: The 1979 Greensboro Killings* (Athens: University of Georgia Press, 1987) tries to straighten out what happened in the streets of Greensboro. Patsy Sims's *The Klan* (New York: Stein and Day, 1978) documents the author's travels across the Klan world and sets down what they said and what they were doing. David Duke tells his own story in *My Awakening: A Path to Racial Understanding* (Mandeville, La.: Free Speech Press, 1998), and a group of anti-Duke activists and intellectuals subject his life to critical commentary in *The Emergence of David Duke and the Politics of Race*, edited by Douglas Rose (Chapel Hill: University of North Carolina Press, 1992). Anti-Klan investigator, litigator, and educator Morris Dees tells his story in *A Season for Justice: The Life and Times of Civil Rights Lawyer Morris Dees* (New York: Charles Scribner's Sons, 1991).

The profile of ordinary Klansmen must, for the most part, be compiled from news accounts of Klan rallies and arrests. The most extensive information on Klan leadership is the Hearings and Report of the House Un-American Activities Committee (1965–1967). Patsy Sims's *The Klan* contains information for the 1970s, and sociologists Betty Dobratz and Stephanie Shanks-Meile provide a treasure house of fifth-era interview material and sociological analysis in *"White Power, White Pride!" The White Separatist Movement in the United States* (New York: Twayne, 1997).

In an understudied field, sociologist Kathleen Blee is the prime student of women in right-wing extremist movements. Her life-history analyses, based on a decade of interviewing, were published mainly in feminist journals. Drawing them together in *Inside Organized Racism: Women in the Hate Movement* (Berkeley: University of California Press, 2002), she does not find women's agendas comparable to those in her study of the 1920s Klan in *Women of the Klan: Racism and Gender in the 1920s* (Berkeley: University of California Press, 1991). Rather, women in contemporary racist movements, of which they constitute as much as a quarter of new recruits, play subordinate roles in male-dominated organizations. *Procreating White Supremacy: Women and the Far Right,* prepared by the Center for Democratic Renewal (April 1996), reprints a broad range of articles, including white supremacist viewpoints. The Southern Poverty Law Center's *Intelligence Report* (summer 1999) contains articles about women's roles on the radical Right and a list of women's websites.

The underpinnings of the fifth era are studied by the contributors to *Anti-Semitism in American History,* edited by David Gerber (Urbana: University of Illinois Press, 1986), and by John Higham, *Send These to Me: Jews and Other Immigrants in Urban America* (New York: Atheneum, 1975). *American Jewish History* (December 1986) offers a retrospective on Higham's work and influence. David Bennett's *The Party of Fear: From Nativist Movements to the New Right in American History* (Chapel Hill: University of North Carolina Press, 1988) rejects an antialien explanation for the end-of-the-century developments. Precursors are to be found in Leo Ribuffo's *The Old Christian Right: The Protestant Far Right from the Depression to the Cold War* (Philadelphia: Temple University Press, 1983); Glen Jeansonne's *Gerald L. K. Smith: Minister of Hate* (New Haven, Conn.: Yale University Press, 1988); Alan Brinkley's *Voices of Protest: Huey Long, Father Coughlin, and the Great Depression* (New York: Knopf, 1982); and Philip Jenkins's "Home-Grown Terror," *American Heritage* 46, no. 5 (September 1955): 38–46. Neil Baldwin's *Henry Ford and the Jews: The Mass Production of Hate* (New York: Public Affairs, 2001) roots Ford's anti-Semitism in the messages learned in childhood from the *McGuffey Reader* and other negative images in the general culture. Ford was a mechanical genius, but a simple view of a corrupt people behind an international banking conspiracy satisfied Ford's social vision. What he believed he never gave up or questioned. He signed, without reading, the disavowal of prejudice written for him, leaving his heirs and the Ford Motor Car Company to clean up the damage to its name. The collected articles from Henry Ford's *Dearborn Independent* in William J. Cameron's

The International Jew: The World's Foremost Problem (Dearborn, Mich., 1920) has never been out of print.

George Johnson's *Architects of Fear: Conspiracy Theories and Paranoia in American Politics* (Los Angeles: Jeremy P. Thacher, 1983) is a valuable source about 300 years of conspiracy mongering, beginning with alarm over the "Illuminati," "Rosicrucians," and "Freemasonry." Robert Goldberg's *Enemies Within: The Culture of Conspiracy in Modern America* (New Haven, Conn.: Yale University Press, 2001) shows how deep a role conspiracy plays in our culture and tells the story of the past half century, ranging across the culture from UFOs and the murder of President Kennedy to the coming of the anti-Christ. His notes include lists of films, media programs, and websites. For an explanation of the role of "prophecy," read Paul Boyer's *When Time Shall Be No More: Prophecy Belief in Modern American Culture* (Cambridge, Mass.: Harvard University Press, 1992). Leonard Zeskind's *The "Christian Identity" Movement: A Theological Justification for Racist and Anti-Semitic Violence* (Atlanta: Center for Democratic Renewal, 1986) and Michael Barkun's *Religion and the Racist Right: The Origins of the Christian Identity Movement* (Chapel Hill: University of North Carolina Press, 1997) are the best introductions to Christian Identity, and Raphael Ezekiel's *The Racist Mind: Portraits of American Neo-Nazis and Klansmen* (New York: Viking, 1995) is the best introduction to the people who lead the movement.

The organized forces of violence are informatively profiled by James Corcoran, *Bitter Harvest: The Birth of Paramilitary Terrorism in the Heartland* (New York: Viking, 1990); James Coates, *Armed and Dangerous: The Rise of the Survivalist Right* (New York: Hill & Wang, 1987); Kevin Flynn and Gary Gerhardt, *The Silent Brotherhood: Inside America's Racist Underground* (New York: Free Press, 1989); James Aho, *The Politics of Righteousness: Idaho's Christian Patriotism* (Seattle: University of Washington Press, 1990); and Morris Dees and Steve Fiffer, *Hate on Trial: The Case against America's Most Dangerous Neo-Nazi* (New York: Villard, 1993). Excellent early writings on the militia movement are Morris Dees with James Corcoran, *Gathering Storm: America's Militia Threat* (New York: HarperCollins, 1996), and Kenneth Stern,

A Force upon the Plain: The American Militia Movement and the Politics of Hate (New York: Simon & Schuster, 1996). As indicated earlier here, the prime sources for the unfolding history of the extremist Right are the publications of the Anti-Defamation League (ADL), the Southern Poverty Law Center (SPLC), the Center for Democratic Renewal (CDR), and the Center for New Community (CNC). Attempting to place it all in a larger context are Gary Wills's "The New Revolutionaries," *New York Review of Books* 42, no. 13 (August 1995): 50–55, and, in an international context, *Encounters with the Contemporary Radical Right*, edited by Peter Merkl and Leonard Weinberg (Boulder: University of Colorado Press, 1993), and Martin Lee's *The Beast Reawakens: Fascism's Resurgence from Hitler's Spymasters to Today's Neo-Nazi Groups and Right-Wing Extremists* (New York: Routledge, 1997). George Fredrickson, *Racism: A Short History* (Princeton, N.J.: Princeton University Press, 2002), places anti-Semitism and white supremacy in a larger historical perspective.

Acknowledgments

*R*ather than using notes, I have sought to incorporate the sources of insight and interpretation within the text and to use the bibliographic essay as a guide for interested readers. In addition, I am indebted to many people, notably Fletcher Baldwin, Henry and Jean Chalmers, Richard Cohen, Edward Crowther, John Dittmer, Joe Feagin, Michael Gannon, Laura Langlie, Meredith Morris-Babb, Marian Price, Mark Potok, Penny Weaver, Randall Williams, Laurie Wood, Anne Wyatt-Brown, Robert Zieger, and Graphics, Circa, and the Library of the University of Florida.

Some of the material in *Backfire: How the Ku Klux Klan Helped the Civil Rights Movement* has been previously published as chapters 46–52 in my *Hooded Americanism: The History of the Ku Klux Klan* (3rd ed., 1989), pages 343–423. Copyright 1981, Duke University Press. All rights reserved. Reproduced with author permission. With editing and addition, this includes the Klan after the school desegregation decision (chapter 2), the Klan's bombing campaign (chapter 3), St. Augustine and Georgia in the summer of 1963 (chapter 6), Birmingham's 16th Street Baptist Church bombing (chapter 12), the 1970s Klan (chapter 13), the Greensboro affair (chapter 14), and more limited use in the accounts of the 1960 presidential election (chapter 4), David Duke (chapter 15), and violence in Mississippi (chapter 7) and Selma, Alabama (chapter 8).

Index

About the Author

David Chalmers is the author of *Hooded Americanism: The History of the Ku Klux Klan* as well as *And the Crooked Places Made Straight: The Struggle for Social Change in the 1960s.* He went to jail with Martin Luther King Jr. in St. Augustine, Florida; was an expert witness in a Ku Klux Klan trial in federal court in Chattanooga; and was a consultant to President Lyndon Johnson's National Violence Commission. He has been Fulbright or Exchange Professor at the Universities of Sri Lanka, Tokyo, the Philippines, Tel-Aviv, and Genova. He is Distinguished Service Professor of History, Emeritus, at the University of Florida.

Art Credits

Page 14: United Klans of America Imperial Wizard Robert Shelton. © Southern Poverty Law Center.

Page 30: Burning "freedom riders" bus, Anniston, Alabama, May 14, 1961. © Bettman/CORBIS.

Page 49: Neshoba County Deputy Sheriff Cecil Price (left) and Sheriff Homer Rainey (right). 1964. © Stock Photo (Black Star).

Page 51: FBI "Missing" poster.

Page 98: Postcard messages sent anonymously to the Ku Klux Klansmen by the FBI in the 1960s. Made available by the Freedom of Information Act.

Page 131: David Duke editorial cartoon. *Fort Lauderdale Star-Sentinel,* December 17, 1978. The dyspeptic Klansman in the lower right is Bill Wilkinson, Duke's lieutenant, rival, and successor. © Marcia Staimer/Artinforms.

Page 138: Detail of the Civil Rights Memorial fountain at the Southern Poverty Law Center in Montgomery, Alabama. © Penny Weaver, SPLC.

Page 156: Klan wife and mother, Davie, Florida. Stan Badz.

Page 161: The Klan repeats King's Selma-to-Montgomery march. U.S. Community Relations Service 1979.